# Healing through Meditation & Prayer

## BASED ON THE EDGAR CAYCE READINGS

## by Meredith Ann Puryear

A.R.E. PRESS • VIRGINIA BEACH • VIRGINIA

Printed in the U.S.A.

# CONTENTS

# FOREWORD

Although anecdotes of healing are interesting, faith-inspiring, and able to capture and hold the attention of the reader, neither I nor the prayer group with which I work have made it our practice to dwell upon names or specifics, because once having given thanks to God who heals all our diseases, we have put each aside and pressed on to what lay ahead.

My burning and abiding interest has always been: What is the Truth behind it all? How does one become a true follower of Christ? How does one become what he/she prays to be made? What are the principles Jesus taught that one must practice? What are the laws of prayer, meditation, and spiritual healing? Can one discover what they are and put them into practice?

These have been my concerns, my search, and my journey. It goes ever on. My desire is to share that which has been gained from my study of the Bible, working with the Edgar Cayce readings, and applying that gleaned in trying to be of some measure of service to my God and my fellow man. I do this in the hope that the Way may be made clearer for others who are also seeking for a way to grow and to serve.

# Chapter One
# MEDITATION: A WAY OF LIFE

"Draw nigh to God and he will draw nigh to you."
(James 4:8, KJV[1])

*Definitions*

What is meditation? ...it is the attuning of the mental body and the physical body to its spiritual source...it is the attuning of thy physical and mental attributes seeking to know the relationships to the Maker. *That* is true meditation.   281-41

Man in all ages, climes, and countries has sought to know from whence he has come, his purpose for being in the earth, and whither he is going. He has found himself enamored of the earth—its physical attributes, the inner core, the atmosphere above, the moon and the planets—and has both adored and abused its resources. Always something within has called his being away from the earth and its creatures, to a sense of wonder and questioning of the beyond.

This call from the beyond comes from man's very nature and is such that he will never find contentment until he finds himself. In order to find himself, he must ultimately find his relationship to his God, as his soul was formed in the "image and likeness of God." The exploration of the earth and the universe is a diversion from the real search; yet, paradoxically, since man can recognize nothing external unless it is also found within, even this diversion will ultimately lead him to himself.

There is the potential within every man to be God-like: creative, loving, knowing, joyous, giving. Yet we seldom find anyone who is living up to the full measure of this potential of being a "child of God." We find ourselves seeking to become more fully human and thus more fully divine, but we discover that we are unable to fulfill even a shadow of the dream of perfection.

---

[1]King James Version; unless otherwise indicated, Biblical quotations have been taken from the Revised Standard Version (RSV).

Nevertheless, we will never achieve that to which we do not aspire. We may become no greater than our vision inspires us to be. If we would be changed, if we would become other than what we are at present, we must set an ideal that will challenge our very soul to be up and seeking. That image of God which lies within as a seed is a pattern of perfection; the more this seed blossoms into the golden flower that it was created to be, the more apparent becomes the unity, harmony, and oneness of the soul with the Creative Forces.

The setting of an ideal must of necessity be an individual choice and effort. God made each of us with unique potentialities and abilities. We should not want to be exactly like anyone else; each of us should seek to understand himself more fully, so that each may become a clear, beautiful facet through which God's light may shine in the earth.

Questions come immediately: How can I know myself, my potential? How can I set an ideal? How do I even know that I am a child of God? Where do I begin? We begin where we are, right here and now. The first premise is: *God is*—the great I AM. God is *all* that there is. We live and move and have our being in Him, whether we recognize it or not. The Scriptures say, "For whoever would draw near to God must believe that he exists and that he rewards those who seek him." (Hebrews 11:6) The Edgar Cayce readings convey this message in the words, "They that would know God, would know their own souls, would know how to meditate or to talk with God, must believe that He *is*— and that He rewards those who seek to know and to do His biddings." (281-41)

We have within ourselves the Divine, the Godhead, the potential of being one with Him. "If we draw nigh to Him," says James in his Epistle, "then He will draw nigh to us." If we do not, He will not force Himself upon us. There must be some effort, some yearning on our part, for the potential to be realized. He has sent prophets into the earth, finally even sending His Son, to try to awaken us from our long slumber. If we do not hearken unto Him and begin to obey, then we—by choice—continue to live in darkness. Yet, there is Light waiting for us:

> "And God said, *'Let there be light';* and there was *light."* [author's italics]                                    (Gen. 1:3)

> "In the beginning was the Word, and the Word was with God, and the Word was God. He was in the beginning with God: all things were made through Him, and without Him was not anything made that was made. In Him was life, *and the life was the light*

*of men.* The *light* shines in the darkness, and the darkness has not overcome it." [author's italics]
(John 1:1-5)

The light which we seek to enlighten our way, the truth which we need to set us free from the bondage of doubt and despair, the hope which will enliven us—all are to be found in Jesus Christ, Son of God, Wayshower to all who seek. This is the Gospel, the Good News that we have from God: that we have an Advocate for us with the Father, One who has shown us the very nature and face of God in the earth, One who will come and be with us when we call, and who will comfort, protect, and lead us each day as we seek to know His way and His will for us.

This, then, is the reason for meditating, being quiet, waiting on the Lord. We are part and parcel of Him, our very being longs to be one with Him, we respond to His love with our desire to be what we were meant to be, His obedient children. Meditation is one way of fulfilling the first great commandment:

"Hear, O Israel, the Lord our God is One Lord. And you shall love the Lord your God with all your heart, and with all your soul, and with all your might."
(Deut. 6:4-5; see also Matthew 22:37; Mark 12:29-30; Luke 10:27)

We show our love by wanting to be one with the Beloved, by desiring to be whole, one within ourselves, and one with God, the earth, the universe—everything. We might variously call God the All, the One, the Way, the Light, the Word through which all was created, that in which everyone and everything exists. The quality of the desire of the heart to be one with the Whole is more important than the name by which we address It.

All the questions we might ask find their answers as we *begin* and as we continue to seek Him; that which may commence with only vague understanding, or even a grasping at shadows, will gradually become that without which we cannot live. As daily, persistently, regularly we seek to grow in awareness of our true nature and our relationship to the Divine, we may not consciously be aware of anything "happening." We may not feel that we are getting anywhere. It is only through persistently seeking, and then looking back at our lives, that we can gradually see desired changes taking place. That which may begin as a discipline will gradually become true bread for us, the very food we find necessary for the sustenance of life.

**Meditation is emptying self of all that hinders the creative forces from rising along the natural channels of the physical**

man to be disseminated through those centers and sources that create the activities of the physical, the mental, the spiritual man; properly done must make one *stronger* mentally, physically... 281-13

There resides within each of us the Godhead—our birthright, a perfect pattern which is part of the soul, a golden flower waiting to bloom. The soul, which is the spiritual body, has spiritual centers resident within its makeup, just as the physical body has glandular centers through which flow hormones that affect the total physical body. The spiritual centers correspond somewhat with the glandular centers; energy flows through them as we begin to meditate. Thus, referring to the definition above, the "natural channels of the physical man" are the physical ductless gland centers; the "centers and sources that create the activities of the physical, the mental, the spiritual man" are the spiritual centers resident within the soul. Meditation, then, is defined as *"emptying* self of all that hinders the creative forces from rising"; the emptying process is related to cleansing and is a long, ongoing one, coming about through time and patience. The glandularspiritual centers, as well as the cleansing process, will be discussed at length a little later.

...Meditation, then, is prayer, but is prayer from *within* the *inner* self, and partakes not only of the physical inner man, but the soul that is aroused by the spirit of man from within.
281-13

Meditation that is also prayer is the silent, healing prayer that takes place as the culmination of a meditation period, after the emptying and attuning processes have occurred. It is prayer *par excellence*—the pouring out, through us, of the Holy Spirit with which we are filled as we come into the very presence of the Divine. Unless there is the giving out of this spiritual energy, it will turn and rend us, wracking us in body and mind.

### How to Meditate

When we ask how to meditate, the real question we are asking is: How do we learn to commune with God? The answer lies not in some technique, though every activity will have some form to it, but with the desire of the heart to know our oneness with Him. To awaken this desire we must feed our soul and mind a more spiritual diet. We must begin to take time to listen to beautiful, uplifting music, to read inspirational poetry and prose and the great scriptures of the ages: the Bible, the Koran, the Talmud, the Bhagavad-Gita. Even five minutes a day with some uplifting word will change the direction of our lives. We must also make some real choices about the kind of reading, TV, and movie diet we choose for our "secular" activities. These choices involve voluntary use of time, energy, and money; they also entail involuntary glandular involvement, because the glandular centers and secretions play a part in every activity of our lives. With every activity in which we engage, we are building toward something either constructive or destructive. The choices themselves may at first be a matter of discipline; but as we continue to do with persistence what we know to do, we will find it becoming easier and easier, because the process of meditation or communion changes our desires, and we begin to want different things and activities than we had heretofore.

Meditation, then, is a life process, not just something we do for a few moments each day. The attunement that takes place in meditation is very much like the tuning of a radio; we tune out static so that what we truly are begins to become apparent even to ourselves.

We must learn to meditate, just as we learned to walk. It is a long, slow process for most of us, one that requires patience—the cardinal virtue—and persistence. Most of us don't want to "wait on the Lord," as we are invited to do in the Psalms. Once we make up our minds, we think that He should present Himself to us immediately, posthaste. And yet, how many of us are ready to come into the presence of our God, now? And so it is, I believe, that He in His infinite mercy allows us to be where we are until we are ready to face His light.

We need to remember here the story of Adam and Eve in the Garden, for it describes the condition of us all: it is not God who hides from us, but we who hide from Him. We did that which was forbidden and then perceived ourselves to be naked and unlovely to look upon. All of us at a very deep level know *all* that we have done and continue to do that separates us from the love and presence of God. He is *here, now, present—omnipresent.* We affirm this; yet, do we believe it?

And so it is that what we have to learn as the beginning step in meditation is to clear ourselves, or "empty ourselves of all that hinders" the awareness of the *presence,* the *light.* I will here outline a technique or procedure (one given in the Edgar Cayce readings, but not the only one that might be used) that may facilitate this attunement. The first step, as we have already discussed, is the setting of an ideal. Just as a person about to begin a journey first makes sure that he knows where he wants to go, else he will never arrive, so we must have an ideal firmly fixed as our compass for the inward journey.

1. Set the Ideal—There Is Only One
   Others, not self
   Love
   In the Spirit of Christ
   Not my will, but Thine, O Lord.
2. Set a Time—Be Regular, Consistent, Patient
3. Prepare—Physically, Mentally, Spiritually
   *Immediate preparation:*
   A—Posture—spine straight, feet flat on floor
   B—Head and neck exercise
   C—Breathing exercise (6 breaths)
   D—Chant—"Aa-ree-ooh-mm"
   E—Preparatory prayer
4. Invite Protection
   Surround self with the consciousness of the presence of the
      Christ Spirit:
   "Father, as I open myself to the unseen forces that surround
   the throne of grace, beauty, and might, I throw about myself
   the protection found in the thought of the Christ."
5. Use an Affirmation
   First, the Lord's Prayer, then a specific affirmation, such as,
   "Father-God, create in me a new purpose: to do Thy will in
   every way and manner."
6. Silence!
   Return to the affirmation to reawaken the spirit.
7. Pray for Others
   "In accordance with Thy knowledge of their need."

We need to choose a specific time and a place to which we can
return day after day; gradually we will be able to sit down and
meditate anywhere, but at first we need to impress our
unconscious mind that we are really serious about our
undertaking. This place needs to be clean, even as we need to be
clean in mind and body. The whole vibrational energy pattern
changes with the cleansing. This is not to say that one could not
meet God in a coal mine, in an alley, or in a prison; it is to say
that there are optimal conditions that we should try to ensure if
we are serious about our endeavor.

It may be helpful for some to play beautiful music before
beginning meditation. For others, incense or the odor of flowers
may enhance the attunement process. Others may want to use
a chant in order to gather and focus mind and energy.

Three chants that I have found very helpful are described
below. Any of these may be repeated three to seven times, or on
occasion for a period of three to seven minutes, to achieve a
higher attunement.

. . . the incantation of the Ar-ar-r-r-r—the e-e-e, the o-o-o, the m-m-m, *raise* these in thyself; and ye become close in the presence of thy Maker. . .                                     281-28

Here we have those incantations that are as but the glorifying of constructive forces in all of their activity within the human emotions that may be known in the present day; for glory, not of self, not of the ability of self, but the glory of the oneness of purpose, of the I AM of the individual for the glorifying of that creative energy within self that may keep the whole body, whole body-individual, whole body as of the group, the whole body as of those within the sound as it ranges from the highest to the lowest of the incantations within; following that known in thine own present as i-e-o-u-e-i-o-umn.                                     275-43

For a group, the rolling OM-m-m-m-m-m-m-m-m-m-m-m, with each person taking a breath at his own need and repeating the chant seven times, is beautiful and helpful at times.

Whether sitting or lying down, always have the spine straight when meditating. The main object is to be so comfortable that one is able to forget the body, yet to have it optimally positioned so that the energy may rise through the centers without being impeded. If a sitting position is adopted, the feet are to be flat on the floor, as a general rule; however, on occasion the ankles may be crossed as a way of shutting out negative outside influences. The suggestion for crossing the ankles and closing one's hands is recommended in a great deal of the literature on meditation. To "close the hands," join the thumb and index finger, put the hands palms-down on the thighs, or fold them across the abdomen with the thumbs touching. This closes the channels through which energy may flow out of the body; and since we desire to be *filled* with the spirit while meditating, containing the energy is highly desirable. Then, for healing prayer at the end of meditation, open the hands so that the energy may flow out through them, as well as through the pituitary. A potential for the ability to heal by the laying on of hands may be detected in the awareness of the heat and fullness present in the hands at this time. If the meditator is lying down, the hands should *always* be crossed over the solar plexus. The lotus position is, of course, completely acceptable but is rarely comfortable for Western man.

It is well to do a head-and-neck exercise as a general relaxant before meditation. Here is a description of one such exercise suggested for general purposes. Each of these movements is to be done *slowly*. The head, of course, should be returned to an upright position after each repetition of the first four movements. (1) Let the head drop forward (and return it to an upright position); repeat three times. (2) Let the head drop backward three times. (3) Drop the head to the right three times. (4) Drop the head to the left three times. (5) Drop the head forward and rotate it three times in a complete circle to the right. (6) Rotate the head in a complete circle to the left three times.

A gentle breathing exercise is recommended to stimulate the circulation to the three higher centers:

**In breathing, take into the right nostril, strength! Exhale through thy mouth. [3 times] Intake in thy left nostril, exhaling through the right; opening the centers of thy body— if it is first prepared to thine *own* understanding, thine *own* concept of what ye would have if ye would have a visitor, if ye would have a companion, if ye would have thy bridegroom! [Inhale in the left nostril, exhale through the right nostril three times.]**
**281-28**

We pray in order to meditate and meditate in order to pray most effectively. Part of the cleansing process is confessional prayer as we seek to draw nigh to our God. Whatever comes to mind as we become still we may take in prayer to Him. As we grow closer in our consciousness to an awareness of His presence, great joy and thanksgiving naturally flow forth from us. If we feel unworthy or unhappy, we will naturally ask for His help in letting this pass from us that we may find His peace. So at the beginning of meditation we may most appropriately practice various kinds or types of prayer, never as ritual, but as a natural result of our seeking His presence.

### Affirmations

Affirmations are encapsulated ideals or short thoughts which we may use as mind tools for building into our consciousness that which we wish to become. We choose an affirmation that is related to an area of spiritual growth with which we are wrestling and which we desire to make a part of ourselves. It should always be related to one's own ideal of what he could be as a child of God.

One should never enter meditation without an explicit affirmation relating to what he is seeking to become. For while the silence is a time of communion with our God, it is also a time for building toward a greater awareness of our relationship with Him, and a period of expansion of consciousness of His greatness, His power, His love, His presence, His peace.

One should memorize the affirmation chosen and then use it daily for a period of at least a month before going on to another aspect of the ideal. One should not use the affirmation as rote, but should always attempt to awaken a feeling or emotional response to it. It is this feeling that one carries forward with him into the silence; when the mind begins to wander—which is inevitable, especially in the beginning—it should be brought back to this feeling or response by repeating enough of the affirmation to recapture the desired ideal.

### The Lord's Prayer

In giving an interpretation of the Lord's Prayer, Edgar Cayce stressed that this was only one approach, one way that it might be used to attain an understanding of one's relationship to his God, to "the Creative Forces." It should be used thus:

**As in feeling, as it were, the flow of the meanings of each portion of same throughout the body-physical. For as there is the response to the mental representations of all of these in the *mental* body, it may build into the physical body in the manner as He, thy Lord, thy Brother, so well expressed in, "I have bread ye know not of."** 281-29

The Lord's Prayer should be used in every meditation, as it quickens all of the centers and stimulates a balanced flow through the whole system. Our desire is to awaken the whole, rather than concentrate on opening any single center, which would lend to imbalance.

It is necessary at this point to have some understanding of seven of the ductless glands (not the only ones) resident within the body, through which the spiritual forces seem especially to work. The relative positions of these ductless glands are indicated in the accompanying illustration. Each of the glands has, according to this interpretation, a specific relationship with part of the Lord's Prayer. In the prayer, the functional locus of the Godhead within (the three higher centers) is addressed first; then each of the centers is addressed in turn, starting at the bottom and going up through the three higher centers again. There is a skipping from the gonads to the adrenals, then back to the lyden, and then up to the thymus, thyroid, pineal, and pituitary; this slight variation from the physical location of the glands has to do with the way the energy flows within the human body.

These different relationships need to be studied and memorized in order that one may begin to "[feel] the flow of the meanings of each portion of same throughout the body-physical" (281-29) each time one says the Lord's Prayer, and especially as it is used as a very special affirmation in helping one attune to his divine nature.

These glands might be listed thus:

Pituitary—Master gland of the body (with the hypothalamus)—
  Our Father who art in *Heaven,*
Pineal—The light center—
  Hallowed be thy *name.*

The name of God in the earth is *Christ,* because He so perfectly showed us how God would look on the earth; and so, the light center is also the Christ center.

Thyroid—The choice center—
  Thy *Kingdom* come. Thy *will* be done in earth, as it is in heaven.

Our earth, within the body, relates to the four lower centers; our heaven, within the body, relates to the three higher centers, referred to as the seat of the Godhead. Each time we pray this prayer, we are praying that that which we hold at the mental level (heaven) may be built into the body (earth).

Gonads—The motor of the body—
  Give us this day our daily *bread.*
Adrenals—The emotional center (solar plexus)—
  And forgive us our *debts,* as we forgive our debtors.

Again, we pray each time, forgive us only insofar as we are forgiving toward others. Do we mean it? Do we wish it? Do we intend it?

Lyden—Center of male-female balance—
  And lead us not into *temptation,*
Thymus—The heart center—
  But deliver us from *evil.*

What we are really seeking as we get the creative energy moving upward from the gonads—the generative, motor system—is that it flow through the next three centers (lyden, adrenal, and thymus) without stopping at any of these three areas and activating them. Hence we pray, "Give us this day our daily bread . . . " That is, give us for today just as much psychic or creative energy as can be applied; and let this energy aid us in forgiving, without leading us to succumb to the temptations that are all about us or awakening the patterns of negativity that have been built, so that the I AM, the real child of God within, may dwell in Thy kingdom, Thy power, Thy glory—forever.

Thyroid—For thine is the *kingdom,*
Pineal—And the *power,*
Pituitary—And the *glory,* forever. Amen.

10

# THE LORD'S PRAYER
# AND THE SEVEN CENTERS

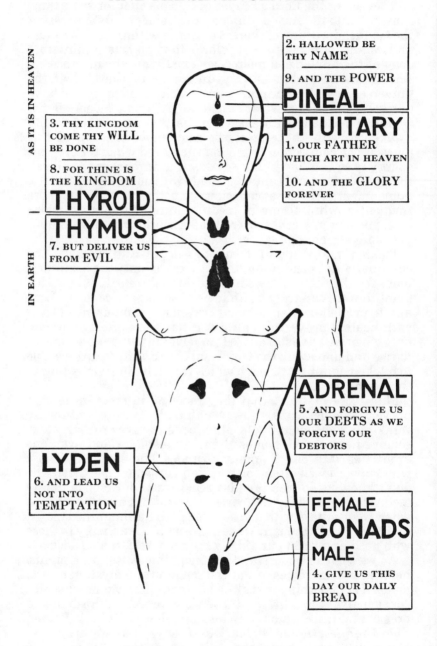

AS IT IS IN HEAVEN

IN EARTH

2. HALLOWED BE THY NAME

9. AND THE POWER

**PINEAL**

**PITUITARY**

1. OUR FATHER WHICH ART IN HEAVEN

10. AND THE GLORY FOREVER

3. THY KINGDOM COME THY WILL BE DONE

8. FOR THINE IS THE KINGDOM

**THYROID**

**THYMUS**

7. BUT DELIVER US FROM EVIL

**ADRENAL**

5. AND FORGIVE US OUR DEBTS AS WE FORGIVE OUR DEBTORS

**LYDEN**

6. AND LEAD US NOT INTO TEMPTATION

**FEMALE**

**GONADS**

MALE

4. GIVE US THIS DAY OUR DAILY BREAD

After using the Lord's Prayer in this manner for some time, some fall into the error of thinking that, since one is addressing the Godhead within, all there is of God is within man. We must understand and reaffirm regularly that man is a miniature copy of the universe, a microcosm existing in the macrocosm. The Godhead within is only an image of the God of the universe. Or, as the Scriptures say, "We live and move and have our being in Him"—we are made in His image. There is the Godhead resident within each of us that is quickened and awakened with the correct use and understanding of this prayer. The connection or union is achieved when the creative energy is so raised within the body that it reaches the pineal, the light center, and contact is made with our Creative Source. Sometimes there is a conscious experience of light; more frequently, what occurs in meditation is at the unconscious level and our only conscious residue is peace, tranquility, and—gradually—a changing life.

Though many might think of silence and light as the culmination of meditation, they are really only the beginning place for the real work we have to do in the earth. It is at this point that we can truly begin to be of some service to our Lord and to our fellow man. Always we should end our meditation with healing prayer, and always it has some effect; however, only when we have so cleansed ourselves that the energy is able to rise and unite with the Universal Creative Force are we able to be clear channels through which the Holy Spirit may flow to those who are seeking.

Many say or think that they have no interest in healing prayer. We must realize, however, that all of us are continually thinking; what we think is either constructive or destructive, seldom neutral. We bombard the atmosphere and everyone around us with our thoughts, attitudes, and emotions. Those who know us well often "pick up" on us; sometimes those who don't know us so well are also sensitive to our moods. As we meditate, we amplify the power of our thoughts many times; when we meditate with a group, the power is magnified many, many times. By thought we can direct creative energy to those who need and want our aid; by thought we can also destroy.

As we come to understand the telepathic power of thoughts, healing prayer comes out of the realm of the mysterious and pious; it is something that all of us engage in any time we send a constructive thought to a friend, a child, a husband, a president. Frank Laubach, in his marvelous little book, *Prayer: The Mightiest Force in the World,* says that we are either helping or hurting someone with every thought we think.

Through setting the ideal and trying to awaken that ideal in prayer and meditation, we are gradually empowered to make our thought more and more constructive and are enabled to set the ego aside more easily so that God's powerful love may flow through us, making us more and more effective in helping others.

## Experiences

Each of us is a soul; we have bodies, and minds that are both of the earth and of the spirit, depending upon what we have done and are doing with them. The very cells within the body have a mind which we have created by our life patterns. The mind partakes of and participates in the carnal desires, as well as partaking of and participating in the spiritual aspirations of the soul. It should not seem strange to us, then, that the body and the mind become involved as we begin to meditate.

The body will resist any attempt to get it to be still and quiet for any period of time, no matter how short. The mind is not accustomed to discipline; we give it free rein most of our eighteen waking hours a day to flit and wander as it pleases. To bring it to a point of quiet, focused attention on an affirmation takes patience and persistence.

Regularly, as we first begin to meditate and try to become quiet, we get a heightened *conscious* awareness of all the things we need to do and have left undone; this is a trick to get us up and doing instead of being quiet. As we persist over a period of time, we may begin to receive pictures, scenes, and sometimes complete scenarios or movies, that are so engrossing that we forget what we are about; these could lead us astray for a lifetime if we were to allow them to continue. The pictures are generally from the unconscious and may contain shadows and half-truths of the past, present and future; however, they are a serious diversion from our purpose of seeking His presence.

Of course, most of us will have genuine experiences of various kinds as we continue with our meditations. There will be sensations in different parts of the body as part of the attunement process. There may gradually come visions and awareness of a Presence or of the presence of many about us. We should neither seek nor deny these. We should be grateful for them, treasure them, ponder them, and accept them as signs along the way, but never demand that they be present as a criterion for ourselves or others as to whether the meditation has been a "good" one or not.

My husband likes to say that he does not know which is better, a "good" or a "bad" experience in meditation. If we have a "good" experience, the temptation is to complain if we cannot return to it; if we have a "bad" experience, it may instruct us to correct our ways and spur us to seek His presence more diligently.

Many feel that it is dangerous to meditate. There is only one thing more dangerous, and that is to fail to meditate. If meditation is practicing His presence, it is the *only* safe activity; at least this is so for a normal, healthy person. If one has unbalanced his body, as through drugs or otherwise, then meditation might become dangerous unless extensive cleansing, working with the diet, and setting of ideals and purposes is pursued with some diligence.

Some become fearful as they enter into meditation. Many times those of the original group who were getting both the Search for God readings and the Prayer Group readings recounted experiences or dreams in which they had become fearful. Each time anyone asked about any of these in a reading, they were told, "Be not afraid, it is I." There are literally dozens of examples of this. Becoming curious about the context of this quotation, I looked it up in the Bible and found the account of Jesus coming to the disciples, who were in a wind-tossed boat on a stormy sea. They thought they were seeing a ghost, but Jesus called out: "Be not afraid, it is I."

So it may be with us at any time we think we see a ghost or have any other kind of frightening experience; if we will raise our consciousness, He will be the one to come. Always there is the promise that He will be near when we call. We should never enter into meditation without a consciousness of His presence and His protection; and with this, of whom or of what should we be fearful? An affirmation of protection that we can use regularly, trying always to enliven it with our faith in His promises and not letting it become rote, is this:

"As we open ourselves to the unseen forces that surround the throne of grace, beauty, and might, we throw about ourselves that protection found in the thought of the Christ." (based on 281-5)

At this point, let us consider some of the experiences of different members of the original Glad Helpers Prayer Group about which they inquired in the readings. These will elucidate some of the principles which have been discussed.

*Q-11. While meditating have experienced a perfect relaxation of the body, the head being drawn backward. Please explain.*

A-11. The nearer the body of an individual, or this, draws to that attunement, or consciousness, as was in the Christ Consciousness, as is *in* the Christ Consciousness, the nearer does the body, or that body, become a channel for *life—living* life—to others to whom the thought is directed. Hence at such periods, these are the manifestations of the life, or the spirit, acting *through* the body. 281-5

In this experience, there is reference to (1) being a channel for the life force, (2) directing this to others by thought, and (3) the experience itself—i.e., the head being drawn back—being a result of this manifestation or flow of the life force through the body.

*Q-12. On several occasions while meditating with the group there was a cool feeling as if metholatum had been placed upon my head and forehead, extending down upon the nose.*
A-12. As would be termed—literal—as the breath of an angel, or the breath of a master. As the body attunes self, as has been given, it may be a channel where there may be even *instant* healing with the laying on of hands. The more often this occurs the more *power* is there felt in the body, the more forcefulness in the act or word. 281-5

In this case: (1) the individual was told that the sensation of coolness (others may feel heat) on the forehead, in the area of the pituitary, indicates the presence of an angel or of a master; (2) there came the promise to this person of the possibility of instant healing with the laying on of hands. Both Hugh Lynn Cayce and Ruth LeNoir have attested to the fact that they had seen this person bring instant healing to another on at least one occasion.

*Q-13. After meditating with the group on April 11th, my whole body seemed to be vibrating to the thought that I had opened my heart to the unseen forces that surround the throne of grace, and beauty, and might, and throwing about self that protection that is found in the thoughts of Him. Please explain.*
A-13. Just as has been given, the nearer one—a body, this body—draws to that complete consciousness that is in Him, the greater may be the power—that is manifested through His presence in the world through that as is brought about in self's own experience. The more forceful, the more helpful, does the body become at such, and through such, experiences. Let these remain as sacred experiences, gathering more and more of same—but as such is given out, so does it come. 281-5

Here the person was told that (1) the consciousness of His presence brings great power to help others; (2) these should be sacred experiences, not flaunted for ego satisfaction; and (3) the more one uses the life force to help others, the more one will have access to it.

*Q-11. . . . Please explain the pumping sensation I experience in the lower part of my spine during meditation, and what I should understand from it.*

A-11. As has been given, as to how those forces in the system are the channels through which the activating sensations arise through those forces of the body for transmission to those portions of the physical body from which sensations are sent out for the activating forces *in* the physical bodies, then these are but the samples, or the attempts of those forces to rise to their activities in the consciousness of the body. Do not force same, but so conduct the mind's trend, the body's activities, as to leave self a channel for such expression.

281-12

We can understand from this (1) that the life force, acting through "the channels," i.e., the ductless glands, is attempting to rise through the body so that it may be transmitted; (2) that these experiences should not be forced; and (3) that the appropriate response is to set the ideals and purposes so that self may be a more proper channel for helping others.

*Q-12. . . . What is the cause of the sensation I feel in my eyes at times during meditation?*

A-12. As is manifest by the activities of those that would bring healing to others, the healing of every sort must come first in self that it may be raised in another. This is the healing in self, with that raising of the vision that may heal in others.

281-12

This person was actually experiencing the sensation of the healing force working in her own body. (1) An extremely important point is raised in this answer, one that we are loath to learn or even to admit: one must be healed within self before healing can be brought to another. (2) This self-healing is an ongoing process, of course, and in other places we are told that in healing others, we ourselves are healed. It is the old, old story of getting to heaven only by leaning on the arm of someone we have helped.

*Q-8. . . . Please interpret the experience I had on Friday night, May 29th, in which I saw colors and heard a voice speak within me.*

A-8. Much might be given as to colors, as to voice, as to the experience that came to thee. As has been given, these experiences come as warnings, as strength, as might, as power, that ye may be comforted in those experiences that at times would overwhelm thee and make thee doubt even thine own self. Know, then, that the lights, the voice, are as the power of the Christ in thine life, *attuning* thee that thou may be a greater help, a greater blessing to others; at the same time encouraging thee, lifting thee up to a more perfect knowledge of the glories of the Lord as He worketh in and through thee.

The lights are as the spirit of *truth;* the voice as the oneness with Him, that must be maintained if thy strength would maintain thee.                                                281-27

(1) The "experiences that at times would overwhelm thee and make thee doubt even thine own self" were conscious experiences that were extremely difficult. (2) On the one hand, the lights and the voice during meditation came as a warning, an admonishment to remain faithful. (3) These experiences were given also as reassurances of the strength and guidance possible when one keeps on doing that which he knows to do.

*Q-9. ... Please explain just what took place the night I heard what sounded like a large top spinning—felt a strong vibration sweep through my body and when I spoke saw a bluish spark close to the top of my head and it felt like electricity.*

A-9. As hath been indicated for the group, for members of same, there is that line, that connection, that point of contact in the body-physical to the spiritual forces as manifest through same. There are the centers of the body through which contacts are made, or are physically active, that at times, at all times, produce a sound. It may not be heard, it may not be always experienced by the individual, but finds expression in emotions of varied centers, varied characters. Thus the experience is that of the broader contact. Thus there are the vibrations of the electrical energies of the body, for Life itself is electrical—it manifests itself in its contacts in a physical being in much the same manner. Thus the experience in self of the emotions-physical being contacted by emotions-spiritual manifesting in the body.

These are, then, as experiences. Learn ye to use them, for they will give expressions in many ways and manners. Seek experiences not as experiences alone but as purposefulness. For what be the profit to thyself, to thy neighbor, if experiences alone of such natures rack thy body—owing to its high vibration—without being able to make thee a kinder mother, a more loving wife, a better neighbor, a better individual in every manner? *These* be the fruits, that it makes thee kinder, gentler, stronger in body, in mind, in purpose to *be* a channel through which the love of *God,* through Jesus Christ, may be manifested in the world. Not as a vision, an experience alone.

*Q-10. Why do I have such a feeling of fullness in my hands when I am holding my healing meditations?*

A-10. A natural consequence of that as has just been given. Pour it out, not hold it in self.                              281-27

(1) In answer 9 we have a beautiful elaboration on how the spiritual force—electrical force, the life force—works through

the centers within the body, even making a sound, which is always there but is seldom heard. (2) There is also given in this answer the *only* worthy reason for such experiences: that they should make us better neighbors, more able in every way to manifest better the fruits of the spirit. (3) In answer 10, the same individual was again admonished to use what had been given to her as a way of helping others.

*Q-6. . . .Please give me enlightenment concerning that which took place in my forehead while meditating Monday afternoon, May 17th, and have had before and since, but of not such a long period, like an opening and shutting of a valve, and was heard by another person in the room.*

A-6. This, as you have knowledge of, is the opening of the centers along the cord of life, and—as there were physical obstructions—produced a physical sound when opened by the raising of the vibrations through the body.

This and such experiences then become *assurances;* not boastful, not overlording, but producing in the positive consciousness the physical activity of which you have a mental knowledge.                                      281-35

We need always to remember that our experiences may be the same as others, or they may be totally unique. Each one has come to this point in time with many and varied abilities, applications, desires, attitudes, and interests; all of these will affect the results and experiences we will have in meditation. Most important of all, whatever comes should be accepted with gratitude and the determination to make of ourselves more effective channels for His glory in the earth.

### *Promises*

As we meditate we become more cognizant of the purpose and plan of God for the souls of all men. As we begin to realize our oneness in Him, our brotherhood with each other becomes more apparent. Our eyes begin to focus and our hearts begin to respond to portrayals of the soul's creation from the beginning and the unfoldment of God's desire and purpose for man.

"So God created man in his own image, in the image of God he created him."          (Gen. 1:27)

If man is in the image and likeness of God, he, too, is creative, a user of energy and a giver of light. We must beware "lest that light in us be darkness." (Luke 11:35)

"For this commandment [to love] which I command you this day is not too hard for you, neither

is it far off. It is not in heaven, that you should say, 'Who will go up for us to heaven, to bring it to us, that we may hear it and do it?' Neither is it beyond the sea, that you should say, 'Who will go over the sea for us, and bring it to us, that we may hear it and do it?' *But the word is very near you: it is in your mouth and in your heart, so that you can do it."* [author's italics]
(Deuteronomy 30:11-14)

The Word, the Pattern, the Seed, the Christ, the Godhead, is within, so that we can become what we were created to be. Paul interprets the above passage in his letter to the Romans: the commandment, the Word, is the Christ, the perfect pattern.

"Moses writes that the man who practices the righteousness which is based on the law shall live by it. But the righteousness based on faith says, Do not say in your heart, 'Who will ascend into heaven?' (that is, to bring Christ down) or 'Who will descend into the abyss?' (that is, to bring Christ up from the dead). But what does it say? *The word is near you, on your lips and in your heart* (that is, the word of faith which we preach). [author's italics]
(Romans 10:5-8)

The *Word,* as interpreted by John in his Gospel, is *Christ,* even as Paul has stated. Christ is Love incarnate. The Word which dwells within our members is the Godhead, or the image of God, in which we were created in the beginning, and which lies dormant, waiting to be awakened by our will; it is the potentiality within for us to be fully loving, fully light-bearing.

"In the beginning was the Word, and the Word was with God, and the Word was God. He was in the beginning with God; all things were made through him, and without him was not anything made that was made. In him was life, and the life was the light of men."
(John 1:1-4)

"This is the covenant which I will make with the house of Israel after those days, says the Lord: I will put my law within them, and I will write it upon their hearts; and I will be their God, and they shall be my people. And no longer shall each man teach his neighbor and each his brother, saying, 'Know the Lord,' for they shall all know me, from the least of them to the greatest, says the Lord; for I will forgive their iniquity, and I will remember their sin no more." (Jer. 31:33-34)

Jeremiah reaffirms the covenant of God with His children, that covenanted potential within each soul to be like the Creator and to know Him. No one will seek a guru, for the real teacher will be recognized from within. Both the Christ potential and the kingdom are within.

"And it shall come to pass afterward,
  that I will pour out my spirit on all flesh;
Your sons and your daughters shall prophesy,
  your old men shall dream dreams,
And your young men shall see visions.
  Even upon the menservants and maidservants
In those days, I will pour out my spirit."
(Joel 2:28-29)

Joel, too, looked toward that great day with hope for the human race to be truly enlightened. God has always been pouring out His Spirit; man as a whole has not been receptive to it. But these may be the days spoken of, longed and hoped for, when the Spirit will be poured out upon all flesh—and received—for in this day there are dreamers of dreams, seers of visions, many who are prophesying, and many who look for the "day of the Lord."

We find in the Gospel of John, the mystical Gospel, the most profound understanding of the true message that Jesus was trying to teach all of mankind:

"God is Spirit, and those who worship Him must worship in spirit and truth." (John 4:24)

God is not manifested reality (except in the perfect example, Jesus Christ), but is rather the true essence of all things. Our true worship must be from within, as we make contact with our true identity and raise that to contact Him, as in the quietness of prayer and meditation.

"I am the bread of life: he who comes to me shall not hunger, and he who believes in me shall never thirst." (John 6:35)

He is the real food for our souls. When we *truly* know ourselves to be children of God, brothers and sisters with Christ, the restless search for the food of the soul is over.

20

> "It is the Spirit that gives life, the flesh is of no avail: the words that I have spoken to you are spirit and life."
>
> (John 6:63)

We will never find the meaning of life, the source of happiness and real joy, as long as we are looking for it at the material level. Once we have realized our true beingness in Christ, then all of life, all of the material, takes on more harmony, more beauty, more joy. But only when we have those words live in us does this become true.

> "If you continue in my word, you are truly my disciples, and you will know the truth, and the truth will make you free." (John 8:31-32)

Only when we continue in His word—i.e., when we keep on keeping on—are His promises able to bear fruit, and we become true followers. As we continue through meditation to "practice the presence" of Christ, so do we begin to know the truth that frees us from the delusions of the world.

> "I am the way, the truth, and the life; no one comes to the Father but by me. If you had known me you would have known my Father also: henceforth you know Him and have seen Him." (John 14:6-7)

While Jesus of Nazareth is the perfect pattern, the Son of God, and while He shows us the Way, we must learn from the I AM within to come into the very presence of God the Father. In seeking, knowing, and loving Jesus and *truly* realizing that He is that manifested reality of the love of the Father in the earth, we are seeing and knowing the Father's true essence: *Love* and *Truth*.

> "Truly, truly, I say to you, he who believes in me will also do the works that I do: and greater works than these will he do." (John 14:12)

If we believe in Jesus Christ, in His promises, in His assertion that we are all children of God, then we also have to believe that the same Spirit that flowed through Him can potentially flow through us so that we may do the works that He did. *The real work that Christ did was to show mankind that He loves us, despite our ugliness, our hatred, our insufficiency.* This is the real work that we must do, not just the miraculous acts which were performed as a result of this great love.

"If you love me, you will keep my commandments. And I will pray the Father, and *He will give you another Counselor,* to be with you forever, *even the Spirit of Truth,* whom the world cannot receive, because it neither sees him nor knows him: you know him, for he dwells with you, and will be in you."
[author's italics]                                    (John 14:15-17)

We will attempt to live an exemplary life, not because of fear, but because of our love of God. We can do this only by seeking consistently, patiently, daily, to come to know Him and to manifest His love. As we seek to manifest His love and abide in Him, then it is that the Counselor, the Spirit of Truth, comes to us, comforts and guides us.

"I will not leave you desolate; I will come to you...
"If a man loves me, he will keep my word, and my Father will love him, and we will come to him and make our home with him."                 (John 14:18, 23)

The promise is not only that we will have the Comforter, but that Jesus Christ and the Father will come to us and will dwell within us. I know many, many "average Christians" who practice meditation and prayer, and have peace and assurance, as well as the experience of the presence of Jesus and the Comforter, the Holy Spirit, and the awareness of the love and beneficence of the Father.

"Nevertheless I tell you the truth: it is to your advantage that I go away, for if I do not go away, the Counselor will not come to you: but if I go, I will send him to you...
"When the Spirit of Truth comes, he will guide you into all the truth."                      (John 16:7, 13)

The first is a hard saying; who can hear it? Jesus, who became the Christ, knew that it was necessary for Him to leave the earth, so that His disciples and those who came afterward would not keep depending upon Him in the flesh to do all those things for which they thought they needed Him. In particular, they thought they needed Him in the flesh to make contact for them with the Father. Only through His departure could they (and we) learn that His true essence is Spirit, that their (and our) true essence is Spirit, and that each of us must turn within to find the kingdom and manifest His love.

Many today, and always, have been inclined to ask, as Pilate did, "What is truth?" The real truth about which we need to be concerned is that God is our Father, Christ is our Brother, and we all are children of the one God. There lies within each of us the potential for manifesting our true nature, by transforming our lower nature to the higher pattern. Truth is the conformity with the highest, or ideal, standard; Christ is that standard.

There are many other promises made to us in the Bible; those that have been discussed here are enough to set our hearts and our minds seeking in the right direction, but let us consider this final promise:

> "Again I say to you, if two of you agree on earth about anything they ask, it will be done for them by my Father in heaven. For where two or three are gathered in my name, there am I in the midst of them."  (Matthew 18:19-20)

Many of us no longer have an expectant attitude. Any time anything goes wrong we rush out to get help, or at least to talk about our trouble with anyone we can find who will listen. He has promised and is faithful. It is we who do not seek. It is we who do not ask. It is we who do not trust. There is no assertion as to when the problem will be solved; but there is the promise that it will be done even as we have believed and asked. We must be persistent in faith and hope.

We need also to realize that "in my name" means "in my nature"; thus, the above quotation can be understood to mean, "Where those are gathered who are seeking to be transformed into my image, *there* will I be." So seldom is it that we find in a Christian gathering any real expectancy that this promise might be fulfilled; hence, there is the loss of power, the loss of aliveness, the loss of hope, faith, and love.

All of these promises can be ours. All of them should be claimed by all of us as we set our standard in Him, as we seek His presence and His power in our daily meditations. He *will* come as He has promised. Will we be waiting? The important coming occurs when He comes to us, abides with us, and helps us to begin to act as children of the Living God.

# Chapter Two
# AFFIRMATIONS

## *Introduction*

We talked about the necessity of setting ideals before beginning to meditate. We need to know the destination we are seeking before we set out on the journey. The true meditation that we are seeking to come to understand more fully is the journey of the soul in its attempt to commune with God, its seeking to manifest its identity as a child of God. The journey is the seeking and the manifesting of our true nature; the destiny is in Him, is oneness with Him.

Affirmations are statements that we hold as expressing desirable aspirations, ideals, or purposes of the soul. They might also be defined as Western mantras, tools of the mind. We know that the mind of man is the builder and might be compared to the Christ aspect of the Trinity. Therefore affirmations, as mantras, should incorporate those ideals related to becoming like the Son. In order for any affirmation to be used mantrically it must be memorized, so that we can sense and feel the meaning of it throughout our whole body-mind as we carry it into the quietness of meditation.[2]

The Lord's Prayer, properly understood, is perhaps the greatest Western mantra. Its relationship to the various spiritual centers within the body needs to be studied and worked with over time, so that we can truly come to feel "the flow of the meanings. . . throughout the body-physical." (281-29) It can be used as a prayer, as a mantra, or, if one chooses to work on one particular aspect of it at a time, as a collection of many mantras (bija-mantras). An example of one aspect of it that might be used is "May Thy will be done in earth as it is in heaven."

When the Lord's Prayer is used as a whole and understood, it becomes the greatest mantra we have for attuning the whole

---

[2] See Puryear and Thurston's *Meditation and the Mind of Man,* published by A.R.E. Press, for a fuller explanation of the Christ as mind, and mantras as mind tools.

body to the awareness of the soul's oneness with God. As such, it should be used after our preliminary preparation and attunement prayers, and immediately prior to the specific affirmation we are working with. We use specific affirmations for a variety of reasons: (1) to let go of those negative patterns we have built—i.e., as a cleansing tool; (2) to work systematically on a growth pattern of the soul; (3) for healing; (4) for working with the dead; and/or (5) as a way of attuning a whole group, nation, or world toward one ideal.

That which is sorely needed in our time, that which is missing in the modern Church, is a presentation of material that will lead to systematic spiritual growth and development. I sincerely believe that there is presented in the two volumes of *A Search for God* an approach that can serve many as the directing or guiding light toward such growth. It is with this understanding of the purpose behind these two volumes that I would like to work extensively with the layout of these books and the sequence of affirmations they present; perhaps following this format will provide encouragement for everyone to use these affirmations in his own spiritual growth.

### A Search for God

There are two unimposing little volumes that the Association for Research and Enlightenment uses in its Study Group program—*A Search for God,* Books I and II. These books were written over an eleven-year period by twelve people who, working as a group, studied, meditated, and prayed together regularly and attempted to live the concepts with which they were working. The concepts that they were seeking to apply related to developing a conscious awareness of their relationship with God and to a balanced development toward the Christ Consciousness.[3]

Included in each book are twelve lessons; the second volume is a parallel of the first and gives a more advanced approach to each of the twelve steps discussed in Book I. The twelve steps or lessons are based on spiritual law and are all aspects of the great commandments to love God and to love our neighbor. These commandments seem simple until one attempts to live them hour by hour, day by day. Practicing prayer and meditation regularly, using each affirmation daily for a period of at least one month; working with a group (or as an individual, if no group connection is possible); and using disciplines to make applicable our progress—these are

[3]These two books are based on the series of psychic discourses that has recently been published as *The Study Group Readings,* Vol. 7 of the Edgar Cayce Library Series.

25

measures that can surely enable us to become what we desire to be made. The use of the affirmations in a sequentialized way enables one to work on a growth pattern of spiritual awareness and application. Indeed, it was for this purpose that they were given.

*Meditation:*
> "Be still, and know that I am God."
> (Psalm 46:10)

Although we have just devoted a whole chapter to meditation, it is important to note that *A Search for God,* Book I, begins not with Chapter One, but with a consideration of this subject. This section is set apart as the specific place at which to begin our search; it is not counted as one of the twelve lessons of the book.

There are three possible affirmations that we might use in beginning to work with meditation. Each has basically the same meaning; each is from a different orientation—Christian, Jewish, and Hindu.

### *The Christian:*

**There is being raised within me that Christ Consciousness that is sufficient for every need within my body, my mind, my soul.**                                                                **281-7**

We define the Christ Consciousness as "the awareness within the soul, imprinted in pattern on the mind and waiting to be awakened by the will, of the soul's oneness with God." (5749-14)

### *The Jewish:*

I AM THAT I AM.
Exodus 3:14, The Masoretic Text

In trying to give Moses the understanding and the courage to go back into Egypt, the Spirit of the Living God gives him the assurance that he, Moses, is His child, created by Him, and his being partakes of the same Being that is the Holiness of the Divine. The *I AM* within Moses (within each of us) is the same as *THAT* (the Divine, which can only be pointed to) *I AM.* This is the same understanding given to us in Psalm 46, in which we are told: BE STILL (meditate), *and know that* I AM (my own being is the same Being that is) GOD.

### *The Hindu:*

"Tat Tvam Asi"

This Sanscrit gem rendered into English would be: *THAT THOU ART.* This affirmation is basically the same as the other two; there is the recognition of the soul's oneness with the

26

Divine. Again, the Divine is unnamed and can only be pointed to as *THAT,* and the soul is reminded that it is of the same substance—i.e., THOU ART (the same as the Divine) THAT.

### *Twelve Steps in Soul Development*[4]

### 1. *Cooperation:*

"Not my will but Thine, O Lord, be done in me and through me. Let me ever be a channel of blessings, today, now, to those that I contact in every way. Let my going in, my coming out be in accord with that Thou would have me do, and as the call comes, 'Here am I, send me, use me.'"

*A.S.F.G.* I, p. 22[5]

Cooperation at the spiritual level is setting aside the lower self so that the Spirit may flow through us, enabling us to be purer channels of God's love to all we encounter day by day. It is the ability to begin to recognize God's good for us, His will, and to choose that path—the higher, the better, the safer, the more fulfilling one at every level. It is being willing to be open to guidance from a higher level in order that our lives will have significance beyond our own selfish desires and so that His purpose may be fulfilled in our world in His way. This is not accomplished in a day, a month, or a year; it is something that must be worked at for a lifetime, as are all the spiritual virtues treated in *A Search for God.*

The warning and the threat is given time and again: If you are not willing to continue, do not even begin. And yet, with the flow of God's Spirit through us as we seek cooperation with Him, we find all of life opening up to us (even through the door that we have called death), to those for whom we are concerned and whom we may aid, and to those who may give to us the assurance of their continuing love and protection.

### 2. *Know Thyself:*

"Father, as we seek to see and know Thy face, may we each, as individuals and as a group, come to know ourselves, even as we are known, that we—as lights in Thee—may give the better concept of Thy Spirit in this world."          *A.S.F.G.* I, p. 30

---

[4]See Harmon Bro's *Edgar Cayce on Religion and Psychic Experience* for a further development of these twelve steps.

[5]*A Search for God*, Book I. If you are interested in joining a *Search for God* Study Group, please write: Study Group Department, P.O. Box 595, Virginia Beach, VA 23451.

Only as we seek our true relationship with the Father do we come to experience ourselves as His children, created by Him to be co-creators and companions with Him. Unless we work at reestablishing this relationship with Him, we can never realize our potential for creativity, joy, and wholeness. There is also a great expansion in our understanding of the brotherhood of all souls as part of God and part of ourselves as we work in the close relationship of a group that has as its purpose the rediscovery of its relationship to the Creator. As this understanding is sought, caught, and lived, there is the light given to those who live in darkness; there is the quickening within others that they, too, may find and know the *Way*.

As we seek to apply the lesson of knowing ourselves—i.e., of becoming what we pray to be made—life opens up to us with hunches and impressions that are helpful in setting our lives in order.

## 3. *What Is My Ideal?*

"God, be merciful to me! Help Thou my unbelief! Let me see in Him that Thou would have me see in my fellow man. Let me see in my brother that I see in Him whom I worship."

*A.S.F.G.* I, p. 40

Because we are all so caught up in and enmeshed in the earth, the very soul cries out in anguish for "mercy" and for a strengthening of those tenuous threads of faith in an all-wise Creator. We have so separated Jesus Christ from His humanity and man from his divinity that it is difficult to conceive any similarity between the creature and the Creator. Yet, until there is that recognition of the divine potential within each soul, we cannot relate effectively to our brother, our God, or ourselves. We cannot attain an ideal of union with God as long as we are alienated from our brother.

Until I know myself to be myself, yet potentially one with the Father, I only grasp at straws in trying to set an ideal. Perhaps the most important step the soul ever takes in spiritual growth is determining its own ideal. In whom do you believe? Do you believe that there is one power, and that power is Good? Do you know that you can relate in a very personal way to God, through the living Spirit?

As we experience ourselves and those about us as children of God, all as a part of the oneness of the universe, frequently we become aware of the force field that surrounds the body and partially emanates from it, the aura. How we interpret what we see in the auras of others may tell us a great deal more about ourselves than about the other person; whether what we share will be constructive or destructive will in large part depend upon the ideal we have set for ourselves.

## 4. *Faith:*

"Create in me a pure heart, O God. Open Thou my heart to the faith Thou hast implanted in all that seek Thy face. Help Thou mine unbelief in my God, in my neighbor, in myself."

*A.S.F.G.* I, p. 46

Until we begin to cleanse the heart of those doubts and fears we have collected through the years, we cannot be open to that pure, undefiled faith that is a natural part of the soul. Even as we begin to seek, the way is opened to us and our faith and hope begin to blossom as a natural consequence of the search. We must continually work with ourselves to let go of self-doubt, doubt in our fellow man, and doubt in our God. Faith grows and blossoms as it is nurtured.

"In studying and applying cooperation, in using the knowledge we have gained in knowing ourselves, in holding to our ideal, and in never letting our faith falter, we are building step by step that which may become living truth in the lives of individuals with whom we come in contact."

*A.S.F.G.* I, pp. 49-50

As we become aware through faith, the inner spiritual knowledge of the Creative Forces of the universe, we become quickened and lifted up, knowing in truth that "His Spirit beareth witness with our spirits."

## 5. *Virtue and Understanding:*

"Let virtue and understanding be in me, for my defense is in Thee, O Lord, my Redeemer; for Thou hearest the prayer of the upright in heart." *A.S.F.G.* I, p. 54

Virtue is based on our cooperating with the Divine through meditation and prayer so that we may know ourselves as we are known. It is the use of the creative force or energy in constructive ways, ways that contribute to the enlightening and uplifting of all others. It is the attempt to hold our ideal and make it manifest in love toward others.

Understanding flows to us as we attempt to live our lives to the glory of Him whom we worship. Real understanding comes only from God as we seek to comprehend the underlying currents in our relationships with those whom we contact: our families, our friends, our associates, our "enemies."

As we work with virtue and understanding, integrity and creativity at both the physical and the soul level become a real part of our consciousness.

6. *Fellowship:*

"How excellent is Thy name in all the earth, O Lord! Would I have fellowship with Thee, I must show brotherly love to my fellow man. Though I approach Thee in humbleness and have aught against my brother, my prayer, my meditation, does not rise to Thee. Help Thou my efforts in my approach to Thee."

*A.S.F.G.* I, p. 62

The real companionship that each soul seeks, yet seldom recognizes as its true longing, is fellowship with the Father, the Creator. "Our souls are restless until we find our rest in Thee," runs a line that captures the longing deep within the being of each of us. We long for an active, creative relationship with our Maker; but seldom are we willing to take the time or make the effort that such fellowship would involve. There must always be the balance between the active, outgoing, loving service to our fellow man and the deep, quiet, inner seeking to know and to be sons of the Living God, brothers of Jesus Christ.

The more we recognize our own nature and our desire for this companionship, the more we should see all people as our brothers with the same need, although it may as yet be unrecognized. This understanding should awaken a yearning for everyone to know the Way, and it should motivate us to be seeking some means to help others experience the love, companionship, and fellowship that we have come so to cherish. We begin to be able to see in the most horrendous acts of others a misdirected potential for good.

Would we find fellowship with God, we must come to recognize our brother as part of ourselves and part of Him. As our awareness of this unity grows, we move in consciousness to the point where we may have out-of-the-body experiences—in waking life or in sleep—at times to aid others, at times so that we might seek help for ourselves.

7. *Patience:*

"How gracious is Thy presence in the earth, O Lord! Be Thou the guide that we with patience may run the race which is set before us, looking to Thee, the Author and Giver of light."

*A.S.F.G.* I, p. 74

Patience is the measure of our understanding of the purpose

of a manifested idea. That is, when there is the real understanding of why anything is the way it is—whether it be in the realm of conditions, situations, or relationships—then we become patient and nonjudgmental. It is only in looking at the surface of any aspect of life that we tend to become angry, irritable, and impatient.

Patience is an active, not a passive, virtue. One must be willing to work with oneself in order to grow in patience. "Patience is an activity of the God-mind within each soul. Its expression involves mental, physical, and spiritual thought and action. Through patience we learn to know self, to measure and test our ideals, to use faith, and to seek understanding through virtue. Thus all spiritual attributes are embraced in patience." (*A.S.F.G.* I, p. 75)  "In your patience possess ye your souls" (Luke 21:19, KJV) is the admonition we have from the Bible. And so it is through patience that the future becomes the present and we have access to many precognitive experiences.

## 8. *The Open Door:*

"As the Father knoweth me, so may I know the Father, through the Christ Spirit, the door to the kingdom of the Father. Show Thou me the way."                    *A.S.F.G.* I, p. 82

The soul of man was created in the image and likeness of God to be a companion and co-creator with Him. Man, endowed with free will, chose (and continues to choose) to create apart from and out of harmony with God. This self-will has created a barrier within man that makes it difficult to reestablish the relationship of oneness. There is within man both human nature and divine nature; the divine Godhead or seed is always there, seeking to awaken, reunite, and enliven the human nature. It is the Christ dwelling in the kingdom, the door that is open, the light contained within each of us, ready to stream forth; it calls to us, beckons and knocks upon the closed door of the human potential that is shut off from the divine light.

Michelangelo captured this symbolically in his painting in the Sistine Chapel: God's hand reaching for man; man's hand reaching up for God. Each man must seek, raising his hand (the creative potential) to be enlivened by divine creativity. God ever beckons; man must respond.

If through the open door we bid Him enter, then we are promised that all things will be brought to our remembrance, even from the foundation of the world. Thus, retrocognition becomes possible.

## 9. *In His Presence:*

"Our Father who art in heaven, may Thy kingdom come in earth through Thy presence in me, that the light of Thy word may shine unto those that I meet day by day. May Thy presence in my brother be such that I may glorify Thee. May I so conduct my own life that others may know Thy presence abides with me, and thus glorify Thee."                    *A.S.F.G.* I, p. 92

Everything we are is the result of what we have done, or failed to do, about our relationship with our God. If we have come to know ourselves as His children, joint heirs with Jesus Christ, then we should be very different in our attitudes, emotions, desires, and values from most of those about us. Our seeking systematically to establish a relationship with Him and to come into His presence with regularity must, by its very nature, be a transforming power within us.

This transformation should be characterized by humility that lights and enlightens the Way for others. His transforming love should enable us to see the beauty in the lives of others and to forgive readily when that beauty seems to be lacking. We should seek to see and magnify the good that others strive to express. We should so live that our actions, our attitudes, our very lives, point beyond themselves to that Great Light which enlightens all mankind.

As a result of being in His presence we should begin to be able to "prophesy," i.e., to speak the truth to others in terms that they can hear and receive, and to do so with a love and understanding that is far beyond our own wisdom.

10. *The Cross and the Crown:*

"Our Father, our God, as we approach that that may give us a better insight of what He bore in the cross, what His glory may be in the crown, may Thy blessings—as promised through Him—be with us as we study together in His name."
                    *A.S.F.G.* I, p. 102

I believe that it is impossible for one finite mind to comprehend that which God did for mankind, and for the world, in sending His Son into the world and allowing man to crucify Him in the attempt (one in which we continue to engage) to cut off that penetrating light that makes us so painfully aware of our own sins, sicknesses, shortcomings, weaknesses—call them by whatever name we will. For there to be a love so great that in it God is able to say, "I can take all your hate, all your vileness, all your weakness, and transform it with my forgiving love" is almost incomprehensible. He says to us, "There is nothing you can do that will kill the Love, Light, Strength, and Beauty that I AM."

The cross Jesus bore was not of His own forging, and on it He bore the sin of the world; yet in order for Him to do that, His own human ego had to be sacrificed in obedience. The one thing we are told that Jesus had to learn was obedience to the will of the Father, so that mankind might know God's complete love and forgiveness for us in any and all circumstances, and so that we might realize that we are not just flesh and blood, but divine beings as well.

We each are invited to take up our cross and follow Him. Our egos, too, must be crucified in obedience; and that which we may do is to help alleviate the pain, weariness, and hunger of souls around us who are floundering. The only glory there is, is in service to Him; we may serve Him by serving our fellow man. The motive is all-important: our goal should be not to achieve glory for ourselves, but that we may glorify Him by our actions.

According to Paul, to present our bodies as a "living sacrifice" is a "reasonable service" to God (Romans 12:1, KJV) and constitutes our "spiritual worship." (RSV) Sacrifice is necessary if we are to bear His cross and wear His crown. As we begin to bear His cross, yoked with the Christ, many so-called miracles begin to occur.

## 11. *The Lord Thy God Is One:*

"As my body, mind and soul are one, Thou, O Lord, in the manifestations in the earth, in power, in might, in glory, art one. May I see in that I do, day by day, more of that realization, and manifest the more."                *A.S.F.G.* I, p. 114

One of the most difficult things that mankind has to learn, comprehend, and experience is the oneness of God. To realize that there is only one force and that it is Good is very difficult when we "see" and experience evil about us. We must come to understand that because we have free will and can choose to do negative and destructive things with the energy, when used in certain ways it begins to appear as evil in itself; and so the devil is born. Electricity and atomic power are two good examples of very powerful forms of the energy of God; they can be used constructively or destructively, depending upon the motive and purpose of the men in whose hands they lie.

Jesus, more than anyone else, demonstrated the oneness of divine energy. He showed us the face of the Father—His love, His compassion, His forgiveness. He claimed that He and the Father were One, and then He demonstrated this by making His will one with the Father's. He declared our oneness with Him and the Father. This we must demonstrate through our choices, our obedience, our lives.

## 12. *Love:*

"Our Father, through the love that Thou hast manifested in the world through Thy Son, the Christ, make us more aware of 'God is love.'" *A.S.F.G.* I, p. 124

All of the other affirmations and the disciplines connected with them lead us to this one truth: God is Love. Love is many faceted; all of the other virtues and awarenesses are necessary to help us comprehend what is truly meant by love.

"Love is that inexplicable force which brought Jesus to earth so that through Him the way back to the Father might be made plain to the children of men. It caused the Father to give His Son that whosoever believes might have eternal life. Love is that dynamic force which brings into manifestation all things. It is the healing force, the cleansing force, and the force that blesses all things we touch." *A.S.F.G.* I, p. 126

### Other Affirmations and Their Use

Literally hundreds of affirmations were given through Edgar Cayce for individuals and groups. This should not seem strange to us if we remember that the purpose of this man was to remind the soul of its source and resource—God. Regardless of whether the person was facing illness, business difficulty, family trouble, personal turmoil, or any other situation in life, he was always reminded that there was help and strength beyond his own, if he would only seek it. Affirmations were given as something to hold on to, something to build with, something to help the soul reestablish its relationship with the Source of Life.

*Affirmations for a faltering faith:*

In Thee, O Lord, do I trust. In Thee will I put my faith, my hope, my all. 262-81

I am in Thy hands. In Thee, O God, do we live and move and have our being in the flesh: and we as Thy children will act just that. 262-82

When turmoils of the day cause us to lose hope, then we must redirect our gaze and shift our emphasis to Him who is the source of all our good.

*Affirmations for self-healing:*

As I seek, wilt Thou harken, O Father of mercy, and in the

promises that were given by and through the Christ in the earth, make me whole every whit—now. 281-17

As Thou, O Lord, art the Giver of life, of health, make me whole through the promises we claim in Jesus, Thy Son.
281-18

Even as we seek in faith, so are we rewarded by His grace. His promises are sure, and when there is true seeking, the finding of His mercy and healing will follow.

*Affirmations for those who seek to be of aid:*

Let me rededicate my life, my heart, my body, to the service of my God, that I may be a channel of blessing to someone, now! 281-21

Lord, Thou who art holy, keep and preserve Thou my every effort, that I may bring to the experience of others and to myself the awareness of Thy presence abiding with them.
281-33

Affirmations can be prayers for strength of purpose and dedication of ourselves in seeking to be of service to others. There must be constant vigilance in order for our desires to be continually constructive and helpful.

*Prayer for those who have passed on:*

Father, in Thy love, Thy mercy, be Thou near those who are in—and have recently entered—the borderland. May I aid, when Thou seest that Thou canst use me. 281-15

Several years ago, when I was active in a church prayer group, I instigated the use of a prayer list; the group even had a list of people who had passed on for whom we prayed. After we moved, the group quickly dropped this part of the list, saying that praying for the dead was not "according to Church doctrine." I wrote to the minister of the Church, asking him why he had not made this clear to me. I could just see him grinning in the beautiful way he had, as I read his reply: "I never did think it did any harm to pray for anyone, living or dead."

Well, it surely does not hurt, provided we pray aright; but it might really hurt if we fail to do so. Death is a taboo subject with most ministers and most Christians; many seem content to believe that one goes directly either to heaven or to hell— whatever that means. I believe that there are as many states of consciousness "on the other side" as there are in the earth; I believe we have more and more evidence that this is so. I have not known many real saints in my life, nor have I known many real sinners, though I myself and most of my friends may tend to exhibit shades of both. My purpose here is not to convince, but rather to invite those of you who do feel so inclined to use the above affirmation in praying for those whom you may deem to be in need of help.

Q-1. *The entity has had the experience of awaking at night and feeling the presence of her brother—would appreciate an explanation of this.*
A-1. This is a reality.
Q-2. *On June 2, 1942, the entity heard her brother calling her—was this the exact time that he passed on?*
A-2. Not the exact time, but the time when the entity could— and found the attunement such as to speak with thee.
Q-3. *Was there something he wanted her to know?*
A-3. Much that he needs of thee. Forget not to pray for and with him; not seeking to hold him but that he, too, may walk the way to the light, in and through the experience. For this is well. Those who have passed on need the prayers of those who live aright. For the prayers of those who would be righteous in spirit may save many who have erred, even in the flesh.

3416-1

Pray for the dead, for they only sleep—as the Lord indicated. And if we are able to attune to such, there we may help. Though we may not call back to life as the Son, we can point the way. For there's only one way. And point to that, that is safe in Him, who is the way, the truth and the light.          3657-1

# Chapter Three
# PRAYER IS NOT A TECHNIQUE

*Introduction*

... prayer is the *making* of one's conscious self more in attune with the spiritual forces that may manifest in a material world ... Prayer is the concerted effort of the physical consciousness to become attuned to the consciousness of the Creator, either collectively or individually.                                              281-13

> "... whoever would draw near to God must believe
> that He exists and that He rewards [with a
> consciousness of His presence][6] those who seek
> Him."                                    (Hebrews 11:6)

Our whole endeavor and attitude in this book is to affirm that God *is,* that we are His children, and that by seeking to reestablish this relationship we come into a greater and greater awareness of it. The relevant Biblical injunction is: "... seek, and ye shall find ..." (Matthew 7:7, KJV) Unless there is the seeking, there will be no finding; God simply does not force Himself upon us. He is constantly seeking us, knocking at the door of our conscience; it is up to us to open up to the infinite possibilities that lie before us. Having given free will to His children and desired companions, He does not renege.

... remember the injunction—never worry as long as you can pray. When you can't pray—you'd better begin to worry! For then you have something to worry about!                          3569-1

When you get to the place where you would worry ... stop and pray! For why worry, when you can pray? For God is not mocked, and He remembers thee in thy sincerity in thy purpose.                                                    2823-3

---

[6] Author's insert. The rewards are many, but seldom of a material nature.

Prayer, like anything else, takes practice; it doesn't just happen or flow freely. The first ingredient of meaningful, helpful prayer is regular, daily, conscious seeking to know *the One* in whom we believe. We need to recognize that we can grow in prayer power and ability to the point where we literally are conscious of His presence every moment of the day. But we must work at it before this growth can be made a reality.

My greatest growth in prayer has come as a result of trying to bring my meandering, undirected, and sometimes negative thoughts under control by praying for myself. In working toward my ideal of trying to manifest in my life what I feel about my God, my relationship with Him, and my understanding that all people are His children, I have come to realize that one needs to seek continually to see the good in self and others; this is seldom easy. Endeavoring to do this takes perpetual vigilance, constant monitoring of one's thoughts, and continuous prayer for self and self's attitudes and relationships with others. Constant prayer for self and others, then, becomes a way of life.

A dream I had several years ago brought this home to me with quite an impact. It was a verbal dream that simply said: "Thou shalt not both bless and curse." I knew immediately what it meant: I had been praying for someone whom I love dearly, but I had also been fussing at him mentally for not doing what he knew he should. This attitude was equated with "cursing," a strong word but one effective in bringing home the message. In effect, my fussing was a curse, because the negativity I felt must have cancelled out the love I verbalized in prayer.

Frank Laubach, in *Prayer: The Mightiest Force in the World,* says, " . . . every thought we think is helping or harming other people." (p. 111) The incontrovertible evidence of extrasensory perception, which demonstrates the ability of some people to pick up the thoughts or activities of others, has great implications for the area of prayer. All of us are being bombarded by thoughts projected from others, some positive and some negative; seldom do we *consciously* recognize this, but it is, nonetheless, truly happening.

Laubach continues: "If you shout, your voice carries barely fifty yards. But when you think, your thoughts go around the world, as far and as fast as the radio . . . Every thought *tends to become true* in proportion as it is intense and as it is long dwelt upon. Thoughts result in deeds and deeds make history. Our thoughts *leap* across space and appear again in other minds, in proportion as they are intense and long dwelt upon. Thoughts are contagious. 'What you whisper in secret,' said Jesus, 'shall be shouted from the housetops.' Yes, even your thoughts shout, though others may not know it is you who are shouting . . . if Jesus is correct, then God has set millions of little gods free on this earth to help create whatever we think about. We are 'sons of God' with a vengeance. Our thoughts are the threads weaving the garment which the world tomorrow will wear. You and I created a piece of tomorrow in our thoughts today." (pp. 111, 114-115)

We need not only to recognize but to assume responsibility for the fact that every thought, positive or negative, may be called "prayer"; we are praying to that which we worship—power, the devil, self, or our God.

**For, what ye sow ye shall reap, and God is not mocked; for the desire, the intent and purpose must be toward the first law as given: "Thou shalt have no other gods before me. Thou shalt love the Lord thy God with all thine heart, thine soul, thine body." If the activities make for the exaltation of the mind, the body, or the position, power, wealth or fame, *these* are of the earth earthy.** 524-2

Prayer, then, is an attitude of mind, a seeking to bring all physical consciousness into relationship with the *creative* forces of the universe. It becomes a conscious weighing of our thoughts against our ideals, a way of keeping ourselves in real attunement with the spiritual forces that manifest in a material world.

When someone in the original Glad Helpers Prayer Group asked, "How can we make our thoughts more powerful that they may do the greatest good?" Mr. Cayce answered:

**By the continuing of concentration of that as we find from our own experiencing of the blessings that come through keeping His laws, His will, and leaving the results with Him. Or, by faith in the power that is entrusted the activity of that thought.** 281-15

Another reading expresses this thought thus:

**The nearer one—a body . . . draws to that complete consciousness that is in Him, the greater may be the power— that is manifested through His presence in the world through that as is brought about in self's own experience.** 281-5

### Types of Prayer

There are many "types" of prayer, or prayers that are used for different conditions, situations, or needs. Because of the very nature of man, our involvement in the earth, and our separation in consciousness from God, we *naturally* use or express different kinds of prayer on different occasions. As we grow in our relationship with God, through Christ, we will be much more at ease in our "running dialogue" with Him and in the form and manner of our expression, both verbal and nonverbal.

*Attunement:* The kind of prayer that I have been most concerned with in writing this book is seldom alluded to by others, but is the one which I consider the most basic and essential in developing an awareness of our relationship with God. I will call it the prayer of *attunement.* It is prayer that takes place within the inner self as one seeks to cut off the dribble of inconsequential trivia and negativity that constantly flows in the stream of consciousness. It is the attempt to bring the conscious mind into a constant awareness that it is *now in the presence of God.* This takes discipline, desire, and determination; it takes constant vigilance, continuous prayer. *Gradually,* with time, patience, and practice one can do a pretty good job of keeping tabs on his stream of consciousness. We are told that in dreams we weigh our daily activities against our ideals and what we have done about them; I believe that this kind of weighing begins to take place on a *conscious level* when we set as our ideal practicing the presence of Christ.

*Praise and Adoration:* When *praise* and *adoration* are listed as types of prayer many people are turned off, saying that if God is God, then He doesn't need this. Perhaps these people do not understand that prayers of praise and adoration are our most natural way of telling God something that every parent wants to hear his child say: "I love you and want to be in your presence." This kind of prayer should never be engaged in as a *form,* because then it is artificial. Only when there is the genuine response of the soul to the magnitude and multiplicity of ways in which the love and forgiveness of God is poured out upon us do we naturally respond with a great outflowing of praise, thanksgiving, meekness, and adoration. We pray such prayers because we can do nothing else; it is the spontaneous expression—verbal or nonverbal, when alone or in a group—of that feeling which wells up within us in gratitude for being aware of His having claimed us as His children and for Christ having redeemed us as brothers, joint heirs with Him.

*Petition:* For the majority of people prayer is synonymous with petition, i.e., asking God for something, anything—whether it be health, wealth, desires, needs, character change, gifts of the spirit, or anything else of which one might think. Too frequently there is the very naive attitude toward God that He is "big daddy," that He should give us whatever it is we think we want or need at the moment, and furthermore, that these gifts should be in the form that we have in mind. When wishes or desires are not granted as by a mythical fairy godmother in the time span allotted by man, then he sometimes comes to the childish conclusion that God does not exist.

At some point we need to come to the realization that we can seldom see the big picture of our own lives, much less how they interact with and impinge upon the lives of others. We simply do not have the wisdom to see and know what we—and others—really need. When we keep our eyes focused on the ideal of being of help to those about us, then our prayers of petition become prayers of letting or allowing His Spirit to work through us: "Oh, Lord, let me so live, this day, that Thy Spirit may flow through me to others. Give that Thou seest we have need of now."

We have to keep reminding ourselves that His will is *always* for our good, and that if we will let go of the tight reins we generally keep on all situations and leave those situations in His care, things will work out better and more smoothly for us than we could ever have imagined! Of course, we do get ourselves all boxed in at times. Sometimes we make bad choices over and over again, and then suddenly we decide to try to let the Lord get us out of the mess we are in. Possibly the very best thing that could happen to us at that point would be to learn the consequences of making all those bad choices.

Walter Fiscus, of *Partners in Prayer* in Fort Worth, Texas, likes to say, "Prayer is not the answer. *Right* prayer is." We must learn how to pray in the right manner, but we also have to learn to live in the right manner, with the right ideals, purposes, intentions, and goals, if we expect God's Spirit to flow to and through us and guide us in the most helpful way. Man has to do his part of the job.

Right prayer involves knowing the condition of the soul of the one for whom we pray; it also presupposes the faith of the one who is praying.

Jesus said: "Therefore I tell you, whatever you ask in prayer, believe that you receive it, and you will." (Mark 11:24) We begin with faith in His power and ability to give that for which we ask; this faith turns to knowledge as we see more and more of our prayers answered. And yet, all of us in some situations and with some conditions find ourselves with wavering faith, and we cry out, "I believe, Lord; help thou mine unbelief."

*Meditation:* Meditation is also prayer, but it is prayer within the inner self, prayer without words. In verbal prayer, aloud or silent, we are talking to or with God; there must also be a time when we "wait on the Lord." This expectant waiting is meditation. We must pray in order to meditate, and we must meditate in order to pray *effectively*. We pray as we enter meditation so that we may bring our whole conscious being into awareness of our relationship with our Maker. We then meditate in order to be filled with His Holy Spirit, so that we may then, in intercessory prayer, act as a channel for the flow of His blessings to others.

*Confession, Forgiveness:* Many "kinds" of prayer may be engaged in as one sits down to meet God face to face. We do at this point whatever is needed; that is, if we really believe that the Spirit of the Living God is going to be present in this encounter—and we should not undertake the meditation unless there is this expectation—then we probably need to engage in some confession. Our lives, thoughts, and deeds of the day probably have not been so exemplary that we could come into His presence without seeking forgiveness for some part of them.

Surely this will not be the only time in which we feel the need for confession and seeking His forgiveness, for at any time during the day or night when we become conscious of anything that we have done or thought that has injured another, either physically, mentally, or spiritually, if we review it, ask and accept His forgiveness, and then let our transgression go and forgive ourselves, it is over and done with. There may also be occasions when we may need to go to the other person and seek or express forgiveness.

*Joy, Thanksgiving:* As we relax in prayer, our spirits are naturally grateful for the time, place, and opportunity to seek His face, and for the assurance we have in Holy Writ that He will meet us when there is this seeking. Thus it is natural to have an attitude of joy and thanksgiving. When there is this welling up of gratitude, serenity, and joy, it overflows into expression, either verbal or nonverbal.

Prayers of thanksgiving are often keys to healing, both for self and others. Perhaps the reason for this is that we can come to a genuine attitude of thanksgiving only when we acknowledge that He is the Source of our very being and the Giver of all good and perfect gifts. While the cause of any condition may lie within us, the true resolution of it comes only by our letting go and letting Him heal us, the condition, or the situation. I have seen "miracles" occur in my own family and in the lives of others because of an attitude of thanksgiving at a time when it did not appear to others that there was anything for which to be thankful.

*Intercession:* In order to invite His presence most effectively, we need to set our eyes and hearts on the ideal, and then we need to wait. After a quiet period during which there has been an outpouring of His Spirit, even though we may not be conscious of this contact with the Divine, we should conclude with intercessory prayer for others and for ourselves. We need to realize at this point that we do not have to inform God of the problem.

I have found that people have either of two attitudes about intercession: (1) the feeling that one has to inform God of what is wrong and what to do about it, and that, in cases where there is guilt that has to be acknowledged, one must entreat Him to change His mind about the consequences; or (2) the feeling that it is completely unnecessary to pray for conditions or people, because God already knows and is taking care of the situation.

Basic to our attitude about intercession is our understanding of the nature of God and our relationship to Him. It is easy to mouth words, which we say we believe, about the nature of God—such as omnipotent, omnipresent, and omniscient—without understanding or application of them when it comes to matters of prayer. What kind of God do we worship?

*Q-1. Is it correct when praying to think of God as impersonal force or energy, everywhere present; or as an intelligent listening mind, which is aware of every individual on earth and who intimately knows everyone's needs and how to meet them?*

A-1. Both! For He is also the energies in the finite moving in material manifestation. He is also the Infinite, with the awareness. And thus as ye attune thy own consciousness, thy own awareness, the unfoldment of the presence within beareth witness with the presence without. And as the Son gave, "I and my Father are one," then ye come to know that ye and thy Father are one, as ye abide in Him.

Thus we find the manifestations of life, the manifestations of energy, the manifestations of power that *moves* in material, are the representation, the manifestation of the Infinite God.

Yet as we look into the infinity of space and time we realize there is then that force, that influence also that is aware of the needs, and there is also the will, that choice given to the souls of men that they may be used, that they may be one, that they may apply same in their own feeble, weak ways perhaps; yet that comes to mean, comes to signify, comes to manifest in the lives of those that have lost their way, that very influence ye seek in the knowledge of God.

For until ye become as a savior, as a help to some soul that has lost hope, lost its way, ye do not fully comprehend the God within, the God without. 1158-14

Do we really believe that He is all-powerful, ever-present, all-knowing, and all-loving, an intelligent listening mind who is aware of every individual on earth and intimately knowledgeable of everyone's needs and how to meet them?

Surely if He has all these qualities, He needs no one to inform Him of anything; neither does He need instruction on how to handle any problem. Do we indeed have a work to do, as the above quotation indicates? Is our job really to become saviors, helpmeets for those about us?

Dr. Leslie Weatherhead, an English theologian, writes in *Psychology, Religion and Healing:*

> " ... I recalled two farmers in India, both of whom sank wells on their separated land, only to find that underneath both farms was a great underground lake. If *A* had put a sack of arsenic into his well, he would have poisoned the water which *B* drank. If he had put—for the sake of illustration—some healthgiving salt or vitamin into his own well, he would have improved the water for *B* also. The illustration goes a long way. To sin is to poison the public reservoir. To love is to strengthen the whole community. When *A* prays for *B* he does not, as it were, make a ball of prayer, throw it up to God and ask God to throw it down to *B* with greater force. He is himself in contact with *B* and both are 'in God.'"
>
> (p. 240)

What we must realize is that man is a user of energy, all kinds of energy: electrical, fossil, atomic, and spiritual. We are children of God and co-creators with Him. Our purpose in creation is to help make the connection between the spiritual energy of God and the needs of others. By praying for others we become channels for the direction and flow of energy and we help them to be open so that they may receive what God has already given.

*The Will of God:* We need to remember the story of Adam and Eve in the Garden: it was they who hid from God, not God who hid from them. We continue to do this in the shame of our nakedness and fear of exposure of the wrong choices we have made. God, as in the Garden, is always calling to man, desirous of pouring out His blessings upon him. We continue to hide because of our guilt and feeling of unworthiness. Although we live, move, and have our being in Him, most of us either are unaware of this or act as if it were not so. We need only to become open to the flow of His mercy and grace to us. Our part in the job, then, is to raise the consciousness of ourselves and others to the point of openness to His will.

We must differentiate between God's will and what He allows. Tom Sugrue came very close to this when he asked about the fall of man:

*Q-3. . . . Should this be described as something which was inevitable in the destiny of souls, or something which God did not desire, but which He did not prevent once He had given free will? The problem here is to reconcile the omniscience of God and His knowledge of all things with the free will of the soul and the soul's fall from grace.*

A-3. He did not prevent, once having given free will. For, He made the individual entities or souls in the beginning. For, the beginnings of sin, of course, were in seeking expression of themselves outside of the plan or the way in which God expressed same. Thus it was the individual, see?

Having given free will, then—though having the foreknowledge, though being omnipotent and omnipresent—it is only when the soul that is a portion of God *chooses* that God knows the end thereof.                    5749-14

God's will is that each of us be reconciled to Him—whole, healthy, living the abundant life; but because He has given us a birthright of free will, He allows us to choose sin, ignorance, and dis-ease, until with time and patience we may choose His will for us. Only through doing God's will do we find happiness; yet, the notion of serving God sits ill with us, for we see it as a sacrifice of our own will. Only in disillusion and suffering, in time, space, and patience, do we come to the wisdom that by doing God's will may we find happiness and heaven.

In intercessory prayer we frequently pray for another and then say, "If it be God's will." If we worship a loving Father, then surely we must realize that His will is *always* for our good; but it is we who continually cut ourselves off from that good. This point is illustrated in a story told by Gerald Heard in his little booklet, *Ten Questions on Prayer:*

> "That remarkable saint, Catherine of Genoa, was once asked at the height of her spiritual power to help her poor little servant girl who had served her faithfully. The maid's husband was dying of a cancer that had eaten into the trigeminal nerve. He was in such frantic agony that in the poor reaction of his simple nature he could only curse God for having done such an abominable thing to him. The abscess had penetrated so far that even the physicians of that day knew that he would not last much longer, and the poor child was terrified for fear her husband would go out of life cursing God and abusing the aid of religion. So she rushed to Catherine and implored her, as she was known to be a giant in prayer, that she would exert herself with God to help the victim. Catherine replied, 'The first thing you must know is that at this

very moment God is not alienated from him, and therefore cares for him more than it is possible for you or me at our very best to care for him. That is the first thing you must realize. And therefore I cannot ask God to do anything for him that God of the immense loving kindness of His heart would not do, and, as He is God, is therefore doing; but what I will do is that when I go into the light, I will take him with me.'

"She is said to have gone out of the room at that time to pray. And at that very time the pain became manageable for the man whose suffering turned from what we call a patheia—helpless torment—to an agonia—a struggle and effort to sustain the anguish. He was able to turn his mind with trust to God, and so he died."                                  (pp. 5-6)

The most effective intercessory prayer is that done in the silence and light at the end of meditation. Then there may be prayer without words, prayer in which the person is taken with us into the light of God and He gives what is needed, as the person is open to receive it.

Some people, in using intercessory prayer, pray for anything and everything and then add, "Thy will be done." This is excellent, if we are praying this prayer for ourselves; it then may become a prayer of surrender, of giving up our own selfwill. However, when we pray for God's will to be done in the life of another, someone whose will is not ours to surrender, we are unable to extricate him from the situation in which he has been all along—at an impasse between the self-will and God's grace. There does come a time when others may "give over their wills" into our keeping, i.e., when they are seeking the will of God for themselves and know that we are praying and meditating for them; then we may pray that His will be done in and through their lives.

... eventually this group may hold—with even thousands of others—such a prayer for those who are sick or afflicted in any manner, and *they to whom the will is given* will receive that they seek through the efforts of these ... [author's italics]
                                                                        **294-127**

God never coerces us; He always gives us our freedom. With our own wills we have made choices which have built desire patterns that have separated us from Him. We have come to call this *karma*. Reincarnation is part of the mercy and grace of God, that through time we might have an opportunity to learn the consequences of our choices and actions and to meet them:

as we have sown, so must we reap. We always have the choice of whether we will learn the hard way, by living out the patterns of that which we have sown, or the easy way, by relinquishing those patterns to His Spirit and His will, and building upon them in the way He would have us grow. Grace is not a mysterious and arbitrary dispensation from God, but the acceptance of His ever-present love. By a process of right choice we may build upon the indwelling pattern (as demonstrated by Jesus Christ) through which the Spirit can flow. Grace works through the Christ Pattern flowing through and transforming that which we have built with the selfish choices we have made. For example, an alcoholic may choose to use the once destructive habit of excessive drinking for the purpose of understanding and aiding others, as in Alcoholics Anonymous. As he mobilizes that urge for the purpose of serving, the pattern which might have become karmic is transformed through grace.

Sometimes we want to stop suffering and to be healed at the conscious level, but we do not want to change. What is the purpose for which we want to be healed? Do we want to go right back and make the same mistakes over again, or do we want to live to the glory of God? We as individuals can accept His will, His grace, and meet ourselves the easy way, or we can choose our own will, which leads to karma, and suffer the consequences.

> "I appeal to you therefore, brethren, by the mercies of God, to present your bodies as a living sacrifice, holy and acceptable to God, which is your spiritual worship. Do not be conformed to this world but be transformed by the renewal of your mind, that you may prove what is the will of God, what is good and acceptable and perfect."                Rom. 12:1-2

In my experience, I have found that almost the only way to avoid being "conformed to the world" is through the practice of meditation and prayer. We are "transformed" as we renew our minds and spirits in His love. Our bodies, our lives, must be presented as a living sacrifice if we are to prove in our own understanding what His will is for us.

There is the question in the minds of many who have come to accept karma, without an adequate understanding of grace, about whether one should even attempt to help others. This question was asked by the Prayer Group:

**Q-2. When one is working out a karma, is it right to try to help that one?**

A-2. This may be answered, even as was that "Who sinned, this man or his parents? That the works of God might be manifest before you!" When there are karmic conditions in the experience of an individual, that as designates those that have the Christ-like spirit is not only in praying for them, holding meditation for them, but aiding, helping, in every manner that the works of God may be manifest in their lives . . .

*Q-3. How do we know when to help an individual?*

A-3. Do with thy might what thine hands, hearts, minds, souls, find to do, leaving the increase, the benefits, in *His* hands, who is the Giver of all good and perfect gifts.    281-4

The criteria for knowing what help we can give are fourfold. We should (1) do what is at hand, (2) do what we are drawn to by our hearts, (3) do that which we choose with our minds to do, and (4) do that which is in keeping with the ideals and purposes of the soul, always leaving the increase or the results in His hands.

We must always be willing to do whatever we can for others at the physical level, but I am fully convinced that our help will be more enlightened if we are praying for ourselves and any others we seek to help. Too often we serve the ego desires of others, rather than their real needs. One person asked Mr. Cayce what he could do to help others and was told that he should get down on his knees and pray for them, that this was the *real work*.

> "Is any one among you suffering? Let him pray. Is any cheerful? Let him sing praise. Is any among you sick? Let him call for the elders of the Church, and let them pray over him, anointing him with oil in the name of the Lord; and the prayer of faith will save the sick man, and the Lord will raise him up; and if he has committed sins, he will be forgiven. Therefore confess your sins to one another, and *pray for one another, that you may be healed.* The prayer of a righteous man has great power in its effects. Elijah was a man of like nature with ourselves and he prayed fervently that it might not rain, and for three years and six months it did not rain on the earth. Then he prayed again and the heaven gave rain, and the earth brought forth its fruit."    James 5:13-18

*Vocal, Group Prayer:* In this chapter on prayer I have been basically concerned with the single individual's life of prayer. For all of us, however, there are times and situations in which we engage in vocal, group prayer. Spoken prayer will be most helpful and effective when the individual praying has a living relationship with his God. Beautiful prayers come as a result of attunement with God and concern for others and are generally spontaneous. When a real consciousness of the self is laid aside and there is an awareness of the oneness of ourselves, God, and all others, there will be effective prayers of concern for the world, for peace, and for others.

There are many times in group prayer when someone is not praying loud enough for others to hear, and when asked to pray louder the person may say that he is talking not to the group, but to God. If such a one is talking to God, he should do so in silence. When one is praying aloud in a group he must realize that his purpose is twofold: (1) one's basic purpose is to edify the group and to raise the group consciousness into an awareness of the living Spirit; and (2) once the consciousness has been raised, the energy and light of the group can more effectively be directed to the conditions, situations, cities, nations, or peoples for which the prayer is being said.

# Chapter Four
# THOSE WHO WOULD FIND, MUST SEEK

"Ask, and it will be given you; seek, and you will find; knock, and it will be opened to you. For every one who asks receives, and he who seeks finds, and to him who knocks it will be opened."     (Matt. 7:7-8)

I believe this to be a basic and fundamental principle of the universe, a spiritual law: If we would find, we must seek. Just as the principle works in all of life, so, too, does it apply in spiritual healing.

In trying to guide the original small group of people who were interested in prayer and healing, Edgar Cayce in his readings stressed over and over again the principle of the seeking individual. Even before the Prayer Group readings (series #281) were begun, this was given in an interpretation of a dream that led to the formation of the group:

... this group may hold ... such a prayer for those who are sick or afflicted in any manner, and they to whom the will is given *will receive that they seek* through the efforts of these... [author's italics]     294-127

This seeking attitude was deemed so important that in each of the first three readings given for the Prayer Group it was stressed.

Those that would then be healed must seek through these channels.     281-1

*Q-5. What connection must be established with those we are trying to help?*
*A-5.* As of old, he that would be aided must seek—even as has been indicated.     281-2

There is humor and yet great instruction in this series of questions and answers given in the third reading:

*Q-16. . . . Could C.E. . . . be healed through me? and in what way?*

A-16. By gaining first that sincere desire on the part *of* C.E. *to* be, *want* to *be,* healed! Then there may be raised within self that that will overcome those destructive forces that are *eating* at the vitals of the physical body.

*Q-17. In what way?*

A-17. By first—there *must* be the *desire,* that can only come within self.

*Q-18. I have four ways of healing. Which shall I use?*

A-18. There must first be the *desire* on the part *of* C.E. to be healed! You cannot create them, no matter what thou hast! *God* cannot save a man that would *not* be saved!     281-3

We are always so sure that we know what would be good or helpful for another individual and so sure that we could be of help if we just knew how to proceed. If we could just learn to appreciate the above excerpt fully enough, we might truly be of much more help to those about us. We must learn to value the integrity of every individual and to appreciate his right to make choices that seem very wrong to us. It is extremely difficult to learn to give others the same freedom that God gives us and that we in America, particularly, have an opportunity to experience. Until an individual has the desire to change, there is no way to force him without infringing upon his integrity.

At the same time that we must value and respect the integrity of individuals by not forcing our wills upon them, we must know that we do have a responsibility to be helpful to everyone in all those ways that are open to us. Like the lawyer who questioned Jesus in the Bible, we often ask, "Who is my neighbor?"

. . . "Thou shalt love the Lord thy God with all thine heart, thy neighbor *as* thyself!" This [is] the whole law, this [is] the whole answer to the world, to each and every soul.

. . . Who is thy neighbor? He that lives next door, or he that lives on the other side of the world? He, rather, that is in *need* of understanding! He who has faltered; he who has fallen even by the way. He is thine neighbor, and thou must answer for him!     3976-8

In one sense, the whole earth and the balance thereof is in keeping of those who know the Way, those who have claimed their relationship to God as sons and daughters. These people are those who seek to do the good, helpful, right thing in every situation, in every relationship. As difficult as it is to know what is the best, it is possible as we seek continually to live in His love and be guided by His Spirit. Only when we have come to understand and appreciate our own freedom and responsibility can we truly value and guard the integrity and freedom of others.

Just as there are things that we can and should do to help others at the conscious, physical, activity level, and things that we should avoid doing, there are ways we can and should help at the level of prayer and meditation, and things we should not do. It is very strange to me that so many feel that they know instinctively how to pray and are loath to learn anything new about it. No matter how good the *intention,* we still need to learn and grow; surely we should be willing to take instruction wherever it is provided, so that we may be more effective.

Having worked with the particular principle expressed in the following passage for a number of years, I would like to explore some possible interpretations with you.

**Q-4. Please differentiate the difference in that we are told to pray for others, whilst again we are told there must be the desire on the part of the one to be, wanting to be, helped or healed.**

**A-4. The prayer for others is as defense against influences that would hinder. The prayer and meditation—and the unison of purpose for healing—is as against an offense committed in the body to be overcome, or made every whit whole by His cleansing, forgiving, His life-giving power. Hence the closer the union of purpose makes that as *He* gave, "Thy *faith* has made thee whole." Whether easier to say, "Thy sins be forgiven," or "Take up thy bed and walk"? The forgiveness, the cleansing, is in Him. Union of purpose for the offensive, or offenses. The defense—rather as the calling of all powers as witness of the position.**     **281-9**

We can always pray for others by sending the light and love of Christ to surround and protect them, because prayer acts as a defense against any influences that would hinder the individual. It is a calling of all powers to witness our position of concern. As an analogy, we might think of prayer as being like a soap bubble of impenetrable golden light within which the individual has the ability to move and be free to make those decisions and choices that are in keeping with the soul's purposes. Or we might like to think of prayer as being like the Great Wall of China, which keeps out all enemies. Unlike either of these analogues, this wall of protecting light is energy that becomes directly available when one is ready to reach out and utilize it. We can build this protection for another as surely as we can build a brick wall for a garden or a home; and it, too, takes time, patience, persistence, and concern to construct.

Let us draw another analogy, one between an automobile and a person. Think of that automobile as being stalled along the highway. Perhaps when it is looked at casually it may not appear to have anything wrong, or it may look like a wreck. Chances are, if it is not yours you would not even consider trying to do anything to it; even if it belonged to a friend, you still would not do anything unless you were asked. If it were yours, you might know how to fix it and you might not; you might want to call for help or you might not. If there were someone in your family who was good with automobiles, you would probably seek his help; if you knew of a competent mechanic, you would get his help. You might welcome a stranger stopping to ask if he could help, and you might not. It would be a strange thing indeed for you to drive up behind a stalled automobile that was not yours and start pushing, without first determining whether you could help the situation with a push.

And yet, when we are praying for others, we so frequently are in there "pushing" with all our might, because we think we know from a very casual observation what is wrong. If a person is an alcoholic or a drug addict, or if he smokes too much, obviously—we think—he should stop; and so with our prayers we ask God to make him stop. Little do we consider the pressures and conditions that have led the person into his particular destructive behavior pattern. The alcohol, the drugs, or the cigarettes may be merely a symptom of a disease pattern, not the disease at all.

What we are able to do effectively when we see a stalled automobile along the road, whether there is a driver present or not, is to get out and set flares around the car so that others will not run into it. Or, having no flares, we might use just a flashlight at night or a hand signal during the day to wave others around it. This is what we do with prayer energy when we surround a person with the Light of Christ, which encompasses forgiveness, mercy, and love; in so doing, we free him to become aware of some of his inner drives and pressures, and to work with them at his own pace.

A mother, having raised a child to the age of adulthood, must allow that adult to go into the world and face it in the strength that she has given him. She no longer has the right to tell him what he may or may not do, or to pray to God to keep him from doing anything. What she may do with her love and concern is to ask God to keep him from the evil one and protect him from those destructive forces that are all about. One is an infringement on the free will; the other is a helpful, hopeful, loving concern.

*Q-7. Please explain why the Master in many cases forgave sins in healing individuals.*

A-7. Sins are of commission and omission. Sins of

commission were forgiven, while sins of omission were called to mind—even by the Master.                                      281-2

*Sins of Omission:* That which we have *omitted* to do cannot be forgiven, because it is something which we have set for ourselves and so must complete. It is not what someone else—be it spouse, family, friends, or Church—has set for an individual, but what the soul has chosen for itself and then failed to fulfill. In the very broadest sense, that which every soul has omitted to do is to become fully loving. We have to learn to apply the law of love in every situation, in every condition of life that we meet. There is always a way of redemption, but there is no way to dodge responsibilities which the soul itself has undertaken.

**In entering the present experience, and in applying that which may be given for helpful instruction and counsel to the entity in the present, know that while the influences from astrological sojourns, as well as those of the material or earthly indwellings, make for urges and inclinations in the present experience, these are those experiences that make for, in the application of that known innately and manifestedly within self as respecting the constructive or creative forces of the spiritual life, what one does about same as in reference to one's own experience making for the development or the retardment. For true indeed, he that knoweth to do good and doeth it not, to him it is evil. He that knoweth not and doeth evil, to him the Father may give countenance; but he that knoweth evil and doeth it, to him it is damnation.                845-1**

Negligence is as much a sin as anything else. It becomes a sin of omission for us when we neglect to get enough rest, proper nutrition, or the exercise that the body needs to be healthy.

*Sins of Commission:* Many times the offenses, sins, are built into the body and become part of the body consciousness. They are built by the mind and/or a physical activity and become part of the life pattern. In order to rid oneself of these, there must be a concerted effort on one's part to eradicate the negative habit pattern. At any time that we can *truly* let go of that act or that pattern and accept the forgiveness and mercy of God, it is gone. Unfortunately, for most of us the negative attitudes, activities, and patterns bring enjoyment at some level, and so we continue to nurture them. Sometimes we ask for help to change, but at the same time say, "But not now, Lord, later . . . later."

Sometimes we so want to "help" or "change" another person that we send and spend a great deal of prayer energy destructively; at this point we have stopped praying and are just meddling. Without the cooperation of the individual we may make conditions very much worse for him. We may send the alcoholic on a prolonged binge by our prayer pressure at the mental-spiritual energy level.

The time may come when a friend or a child of yours, now grown, may ask for your help and your prayers to heal some condition or to avoid certain situations; when that happens, you may give everything you have to give by way of help, sending white light and energy directly to him to strengthen his own resolve. This is the "union of purpose for healing." Whenever anyone asks, conditions are completely different and you may use the prayer light and energy differently; the person has begun to seek, and you, with the power of God, can begin to help him find that for which he is seeking.

**Who may make intercession? They that have within their consciousness a channel to the throne of grace, that there may be given into the mind and activities of the soul of this entity those influences that may bring the changes in the experience of this body.** 496-1

Any time an individual recognizes his need and says, "I am ready to change, will you help me?" or "I am sick, will you pray for me?" we can begin to use the prayer energy, the white light, like a laser beam, directing it in a straight line to the body-mind-soul of the person; this is different from using the energy to build a circle of protection, like the flares we can set around the stalled car in our analogy, around someone who has not asked for our help. At the moment of the invitation, we may get behind his automobile and push.

**. . . for ye are *raising* in meditation actual *creation* taking place within the inner self!** 281-13

An individual or a group should first meditate for attunement of the self; when this has been achieved and there has been a period of silence for the cleansing "creation" within, the energy may be directed to others, by thought, using the full name of each person who has asked to be a "target." In order to cooperate fully, this person should be meditating/praying at the same time, seeking an attunement with the Creative Forces so that the light energy can quicken the Spirit within him, which in turn does the work of "actual creation," healing, within his own body-mind.

**How does prayer reach the throne of mercy or grace, or that from which it emanates? From itself! Through that of *crucifying, nullifying,* the carnal mind and opening the mental in such a manner that the Spirit of Truth may flow in its psychic sense, or occult force, into the very being, that you may be one with that from which you came!** 364-10

The *name-target-laser-beam principle* may be used effectively with anyone, whether or not you know him, provided he *says he needs help.* Its real effectiveness depends upon the receptivity of the individual at every level, conscious and subconscious, and upon your own attunement in meditation.

There is ever, then—in thy material associations, in thy seeking for help, love, health, understanding for thy brother—*something,* some effort on their part as well as *thine.* But "Where two or three are gathered together in my name, there will I be in the midst of them."

These are the influences that all must realize, if they would understand, if they would comprehend, if they would contemplate, if they would seek—that ye cannot give that which ye do not possess. If ye have that love in the Christ, in the giving ye have the more; even as He demonstrated in the giving of life that ye might have life more abundantly, that there might be a closer walk with Him. And as ye walk, ye talk with Him, He talks with thee.                    5749-16

The reason this method of direct prayer must be utilized only with those who are seeking is that the energy which is sent activates the already existing desire patterns that the person is holding. If the person's real desire is for drugs, alcohol, or cigarettes, this is the pattern that is energized. This is why, when a person says he wants to change but is not able to work on the change effectively because of the strength of the desire pattern already built, it may still be better to pray for him by surrounding him with light and love. If one is really seeking and desiring to be whole, then this is the pattern that is energized. Such a person should pray for himself, not just daily, but minute by minute whenever the temptation of negativity, illness, or self-destruction begins to emerge.

There are many who at this point will say, "You're dead wrong. As long as the person says he wants to change and we say 'Thy will be done,' we can pray directly for that person." Yes, we may do anything, for God surely has given us free will. Again, I would plead for each person to cultivate an awareness of his own developing sensitivity, so that he can intuitively know and do what is needed. At times I have gone along for months praying directly for someone who has requested my prayers, and then I have found myself shifting gears and surrounding that person with light. Why? Just a feeling I have had. Later this may or may not have been confirmed as what was necessary at that time. Again, I would like to emphasize at this point that simply saying "Thy will be done" rarely makes the prayer an act of surrender. If we send the prayer energy in one direction and simply tack this phrase on as a formula, it is not effective.

Another way of conceiving what happens with direct prayer is to recall the example of Catherine of Genoa, of lifting into the light those who are seeking. When we are meditating with a group or alone and we come to the time of intercession, then we may bring those who have asked into that light or enlightened state where we are. Some may think that this is the same process as the laser-beam principle, simply conceived of in a different way. Indeed it may be; I do not know at this point in time. I know that sometimes, with some individuals, I send the energy in one way; and with others, I do it the other way. I am not sure whether there is an actual difference, or one that exists simply in my own conception.

There is yet another process that I work with on some rare occasions. I utilize this method only under *all* the following conditions: I know the person extremely well; I am aware of his ideals and purposes; I have been specifically requested to "meditate for" him; and I have made very sure that he understands what this process involves. In using this method of sending healing energy, I take the other person with me, both by full name and by sensing the consciousness of his presence, through the entire course of my prayer and meditation—from the very beginning of my Bible-reading attunement process, through the steps of using the affirmation and entering the silence, and finally into the healing period. This is work; it takes concentration and real effort. I must be very sure of my own attunement and balance, sure that the light into which I take the person will not be darkness. Perhaps as I grow in my own attunement and in faith I will be able to do more work at this level.

I have talked with others in my Prayer Group and have found that they frequently have the same experience I do, one in which my meditation period is unsatisfactory, my attunement does not seem good, and yet, when we come to the intercessory period, something happens. There seems to be a shifting of gears, and with the real invitation for the Holy Spirit to come and work through us so that those who seek may be helped, there comes an awareness that it is so.

Now this is the very thing that I am hinting at in relation to "meditating for" another, in the sense of taking him all the way through the whole meditation with you. Unless you are relatively certain that you will be able to make that attunement and have a helpful period of silence, it will be more beneficial to wait until the intercessory period to begin to pray for those who are seeking.

# Chapter Five
# WHY WORK IN
# A PRAYER GROUP?

## The Group Itself

There is innate within each of us that which is creative, healing, and life-giving. For some people, there comes the desire to make this a more active, more vital part of the flow of their lives; hence some become doctors and nurses, some become volunteers working in various capacities dealing with the healing arts. Others find themselves drawn more toward working with prayer, meditation, and spiritual healing. Each should complement the others, for as we find ourselves to be souls with minds and flesh bodies, we have to deal with each of our components at its own level. We must always do what we know is right for us to do at the physical level, seeking at the same time all the mental guidance and spiritual help we can get.

Some will find themselves working in Church prayer groups; this is good and beautiful when there is that real seeking within each one to reach his own optimum spiritual growth so that he may give light and love to those who seek aid through the group. Such a group may surely become a beacon of light within the Church, the community, and the world.

I feel that we within the A.R.E. are especially blessed, because we have as the very core of the "work" the Search for God Study Groups, which are especially designed for individual spiritual growth, for selfless development toward the Christ Consciousness. Since 1956, my husband and I have worked together with a small group of six to twelve people, a Study Group that has met weekly in our home for the purpose of coming to understand and then apply the teachings of Jesus Christ.

I sincerely believe that one cannot be effective in working with prayer and meditation for healing unless one is working just as hard, or harder, on developing a living relationship with the Spirit of God. And so my advice to those within the A.R.E. has always been and will continue to be: join and participate fully in a Search for God Study Group. One should work through at least Book I of *A Search for God* with a group and be progressing through Book II before ever considering becoming a part of a prayer group. Even when a person is involved with such a prayer group, the Search for God group work should continue.

Every Search for God Study Group has as a basic part of its format prayer and meditation together each week and a daily period of individual prayer and meditation; the latter activity is performed by each member at the same time and, like the group sessions, always culminates in healing prayer. If, after having participated in such a group consistently for at least a couple of years, one still feels the desire to do more work at the prayer-healing level, he might legitimately think of also becoming involved with a prayer group.

## Singleness of Purpose

Our vision and purpose must be worthy of the task before us. As each one joins a prayer group his desire should be that he may serve his God by being and giving *light* to a waiting world. The common purpose should be that, through the power of the Christ, one may give that which is needed in the lives of those who seek through the group. Working in such a group, one must constantly keep before himself the hope that each has come together for some definite purpose other than that of self-indulgence, self-gratification, or self-exaltation. The one common purpose should be *to be a manifestation of His love* in this particular experience, seeking to lose self in love and service to others.

When one first joins or forms a group, there is the intention of strengthening each other, encouraging each to grow to the fullest of his potential, and working at the disciplines of daily prayer and meditation. While this always remains as part of the purpose, it becomes a fact rather than a hope when the group works together over a period of years, keeping their ideals and purposes firmly fixed.

It should not at all surprise us that there is difficulty in praying and meditating in or with a new group. So many different ideas, patterns, and vibrations are brought into the group by the various members that it takes time and effort to harmonize these and to smooth out the rough edges. I feel that there are occasions when a group needs to be closed (i.e., not admitting any new members) for a period of time, until the basic membership has had time to work together and become a solid unit. When this truly happens, then others may come into the group and it will not be disrupted.

As the members grow together toward the ideal, they discover not only that meditating together becomes easier, but also that participation in the group provides a real enhancement of the individual attunement which is achieved during the individual prayer time. The group becomes a real source of strength for each member that may be and is drawn upon during the rest of the week when they are not together.

The Glad Helpers Prayer Group, which has been meeting weekly since 1931 and of which I have been a part since 1969, is the strongest group that I have ever been involved with. We are always open to a constant flow of visitors, and when the group is really together there is no disturbance whatsoever. There have been occasions when members were disturbed; when this has occurred, I have wondered if it were not caused more by our lack of faithfulness and attunement than by what someone else brought to the group. We must seek to achieve peace within ourselves, for this is the bedrock upon which we build a consciousness of His presence.

... more and more must there be the united effort in each to bring the consciousness of that oneness of the peace that He gave; who is the author and the finisher of the faith, through which healing may come—by the very application in the individual lives of that peace as He gave. "Not as the world gives peace, but my peace," that is the consciousness of being at-one in purpose, in intent, in desire of the Father; who is the life and who is [He] in whom we live and move and have our being.

Then as each of the group in their desire and their application of same in their daily walks before men make such a united effort, they may bring to others more and more of that consciousness that He lives, that He walks and talks with those that would seek to have His presence abiding with them day by day ...

Then as ye make the life, the love, the awareness of the Christ Consciousness in the Father in thy daily life, more and more are ye able to give that which will bring into the experiences of others that same awareness.

For thoughts are things, and the Mind is the Builder. But if ye fill thy mind with the cares of the world day by day, ye may not in the moment give the best that is in the life of those that live the Christ-life—even as Jesus gave the new commandment, "that ye love one another."                    281-39

When we come together as a group, we must come in love for one another, seeking to lay aside all feelings of unworthiness and knowing that, as we seek to be one with Him, His Spirit can and will flow through us because of our desire to be of help to others.

60

*Mrs. Cayce:... we seek at this time a clearer understanding of the healing forces and their interaction through us as members of this group ...*

Mr. Cayce:... In seeking to be a channel of blessing to others through such a group, well that individually all self-condemnation be laid aside, that self be wholly free in that source of power as would bring hope, faith, confidence, and *healing* to those who seek through this channel to be made more aware of His love in their lives. Not in arrogance by any one; rather seek through meditation, singleness of purpose, to be guided in that channel in which each may *be* a channel of blessing to those who seek.

In this manner may ye know the way; for, as has been given, "I go—and the *way* ye know." The manner in which each may know they are *in* attune, is the ability to feel that consciousness of the sincere desire *within* to be a blessing, *a* channel, to some one.                               281-3

More and more as the group works together, seeking through prayer and meditation to be a channel of blessing in the lives of others, there will be confirmation of the effectiveness of their efforts. Always this should be received with gratitude and thanksgiving that His glory may be known more and more in the lives of others. We should also realize that the daily choice of seeking to be of service gives an ever greater opportunity to be of service. Only as we do the little things do the bigger things become open to us.

... let each know: As good has been accomplished in the lives and the experiences of those they have sought to help, this should be to each as a verification of the promises that have been given, "As ye ask in my name, believing, that shall be accomplished in the experiences of those that seek to know my face."

In the work, then, let each thing be done in order, and keeping that humbleness of spirit, that *oneness of purpose,* that *desire to see in those that seek through such channels the glorifying of the consciousness of the Christ Spirit dwelling with each.*

Let each, then, be not slothful in the activities; not negligent, but·rather let each be up and doing, with a mind to serve in whatsoever channel or manner the opportunity presents itself; knowing that *as ye have been chosen and as ye choose* to magnify His name in the earth, *this choice of thyself gives with same a greater opportunity of service,* that the choice that thou art chosen of Him to be a light in His name carries with it those obligations in self, that thou will be true to the trust, to the service, to those activities that become one that would be a glad helper in His name. [author's italics]                281-22

Because choice is a faculty of the soul, a God-given gift to man, it is only when we choose Him, His ways, that He then chooses us as channels for His work in the earth. As we learn to trust and have more and more faith in God through Christ, we become more helpful to those we seek to aid. This concept comes through loud and clear in this message, which was received through Edgar Cayce in one of the earliest Prayer Group readings:

In seeking for understanding, let each harken to what *He* has to say:

Come, my children, lift up thine hearts that *I* may enter in. As ye have chosen me, so have I chosen you, that ye may be a blessing to those who seek in *my* name to *know* the truth as may be magnified in *their* lives through *thine* aid in me. Grace, mercy and peace, is given to those thou asketh for in the proportion as thy trust, thy faith, is *in* me. As ye seek through raising in self that image of love in Him, so *may* thine self be lifted up, and the understanding come *to* him who *seeks* for same.                                                                                    281-2

There is always a question in the minds of some about how to pray in a group, how to become of one mind and purpose. The key seems to be the *desire* of the individual.

*Q-28. Does it mean we all in the group should hold the same prayer in the same way?*

A-28. Each in their *own* way, but the purpose, the aim, ONE, the desire ONE; for, as just given, to *some* the song of the spheres is necessary for their comfort—to another the beauties in the sunset, in the water, or how, yet all are *acknowledging* the power of the Christ in the activating forces of nature, life, material, itself! KNOW NOTHING BUT CHRIST, AND HIM CRUCIFIED!                         281-8

More and more should there be that concerted effort for the prayer to be one of unison; for, as given, there must be *oneness* of purpose. Even as the Father and the Son are one, "ye may be one in me," if thine aim, thine desire, is in Him.      281-8

It seems to be a condition of man in the earth that in all relationships with other people, particularly in group work, there are difficulties that must be worked out, worked through, if the purpose of that group is to come to fruition. Part of the cleansing, healing process that goes on within ourselves and has results that we can then give out for the benefit of others is a continual reexamination and rededication of our own desires, intentions, purposes, faith, and application of known laws. The question each person must be concerned with is not what someone else should do, but what he himself can do to improve conditions within himself and within the group so that the harmony and attunement necessary for the real work to proceed can be brought about.

*Q-12. As a group, are we reaching that consciousness of His presence in healing, which should come to the group to make their selves one in purpose? If not, how?*
A-12. This, as we find, as a group has been rather of the spasmodic nature. Individuals have been raised high; others have been lacking, or lax, in cooperative measures—yet much has been, may be, accomplished. Faint not, nor find fault not, one with another. *Pray,* rather, one with another.     281-4

. . . well that each take stock of themselves as related to the activities that would be brought about in the minds and hearts of those they would aid. In unison of purpose is their strength. In the prayer of those that would aid comes strength *with* that unison of purpose in Him. As there come those periods when those seeking are aided, give thanks! Are there those periods when those seeking falter, look within—and find that in self that would be changed, *finding* the fault rather in self than in others; for let each have this as their guide, "Others may do as they may, but for me I will serve the living God." *Through* the promises in Him that gave, "What ye ask in my name that will the Father give you, that I may be glorified in you."     281-9

### Where Two or Three Are Gathered

*Q-1. Is group action more effective than individual, and if so, why?*
A-1. "Where two or three are gathered in my name, I am in the midst of them." These words were spoken by Life, Light, and Immortality, and are based on a law. For, in union is strength. Why?
Because as there is *oneness of purpose, oneness of desire,* it becomes motivative within the active forces or influences of a body. The multiplicity of ideas may make confusion, but added cords of strength in one become of the nature as to increase the *ability* and influence in every expression of such a law. [author's italics]     281-24

We must remember that *name* means *nature,* for the animals were named originally by Adam to indicate the nature of each one. If we would meet together "in His name," we should be meeting to make manifest the nature of Jesus Christ. When this is so, He will be present in our midst and our weaknesses may be laid aside in His strength.

. . . one may not hear the prayer or the thought sent by an individual whose attunement is not sufficient to raise that vibration in an individual, but the combined—as we have in numbers—raise to such an extent that the *awakening* comes by this *continuing* of this direction of the spiritual forces to an individual; even as the small drop may wear away the *hardest* stone.                                                              281-4

While it is true that one may not hear the prayer or thought sent out by an individual whose whole attunement is not sufficient, there should come a time when the attunement has grown to the point where it may very definitely be felt and/or heard; as this happens, daily individual prayer and meditation becomes more effective. Another result of this development is that the individual becomes an even more powerful channel within a group, because the energy is multiplied by the concerted effort of the group. No matter how "powerful" the group becomes, the result will always depend upon the response made by the one seeking aid. It depends upon the seeker's faith, hope, and ability to let go of whatever conditions are binding him. We may see the truth of his wholeness; but unless he, too, can see and accept it, it is not truth for him.

**The *concerted* effort on the part of a group merely accentuates that as a force, or power, that may manifest in or through an individual, or as respecting a circumstance. Hence the activity must be as much on the part of one seeking aid through such a channel.                                    281-5**

Group work will always be enhanced when the participants approach the meeting time with the right attitude and purpose:

**That with which each individual approaches such an hour is how much each may put into same and get out of same, and do good unto others.**
**First, let each enter into its own inner self and ask for direction, and—*believing* His presence will be with thee. For, He has promised, "Where two or three are gathered together in *my* name, *there* I will be in the midst of them."**
**Let each, then, so consecrate, so dedicate that hour, that period, to such a service for its fellow man, seeking, knowing, that His presence will be with thee. Then, when *He* has directed thine group, who—*who*—would question same?**
                                                              **281-20**

### A Promise, a Threat

In the very first reading that was given for the Prayer Group the members were warned that the task to be undertaken was a mighty one, one not to be taken lightly, one that should be continued once the choice was made and "the face set in that direction ... " (281-1) This is no less true for us today than it was for them. This work carries for each of us both a promise and a threat: the promise of the greatest fulfillment possible for a soul, for "he that serves another with a singleness of purpose, of glory to the Father, lendeth unto the Lord" (281-22); a threat, because a choice made and not carried out becomes for the soul a sin of omission, which can be erased only through fulfillment.

Each as are gathered here are fitted in their own particular way for a portion of that work designated by the group as the healing group. Hence, when once chosen, and the face set in that direction, that as the warning, as the threat.

In each experience of the individuals gathered here, they— the individuals—have contacted various other individuals in experiences in life, some for weal, some for woe, as has been designated to each in those experiences where either development or retardment has been the portion of that individual experience. As these individuals, then, have contacted others, these have that karma, that experience to be worked out together for some definite purpose other than that of self-indulgence, self-gratification, or self-exaltation. In some this has been the last experience. Hence there is seen that there will be those characterizations in the associations when turned to earthly conditions. Then there are those experiences with the group as a whole where the greater portion have worked together for the common good of all.

281-1

It is my sincere belief, borne out by my twenty years of experience in group work, that these statements are true of every group, of every nature. That is, there are always some individuals who have at some time worked both with and against each other. Thus there will be times when all will go smoothly, other times when some members of the group will be at odds with each other. The only way to overcome this is continually to go back and reaffirm the group purpose and ideal and pray for oneself and the one with whom the difficulty arises.

Group work has another aspect that carries both a promise and a threat—the sensitivity to one another that is developed among the members. In working with a group we are influenced by each other's strengths and we become vulnerable to each other's weaknesses. We must continually pray for ourselves that we may be our own best selves, bring out the best in others, and be protected from the negativity of ourselves and others. Messages may come through for each other; but we must always weigh these, comparing them to our highest ideals, to make sure they are true and helpful. We must also look at each message to make sure it is not more applicable to ourselves than it is to the other person.

*Q-11. Please explain just what was meant by the following given in a reading of September 20, 1931, regarding this group: "For as each of these gather as a body for aid to another, there will be from time to time a message from one to another. This is not only a promise, it's a threat! Be mindful of it, but faithful to each as they are received."*

A-11. As there are the messages, or those feelings that come, as the activity of the Spirit in the experiences of each individual these come. Those that are faithful to give to others that as received are then carrying forward that which has been taken as an obligation in becoming a channel of blessing through which the Spirit Forces may manifest in their relationships one to another. As to the threat that has been given, "He that putteth his hand to the plow and turns back is worse than the infidel," or, as was given by Him, as Master among men, "He that would offend one of these, the least of my little ones, better that a millstone were hanged about his neck and he were cast into the depths," or he that having taken on a vow and then is unfaithful to same, when the last estate of that entity is seen it is worse than the first; but be thou faithful. As each uses those talents, those abilities, the understanding will come—for, as has been given, each have been *chosen* of Him, and each have their own duty as relation one to another, as a group, to perform in that undertaken.                  281-6

## Not a Gossip Session

More prayer groups have disintegrated because of this one factor (gossip) than any other. The intention may be sincere, the desire may be to help, but when discussion of others' problems, conditions, or situations begins to be brought into the conversation within the group, the seeds of dissolution are there.

The most important thing to know is that it is *not necessary* to know why another person wants prayer. Most frequently what the person thinks is wrong is not the real problem anyway; most prayer requests are for healing of symptoms, and symptoms can be and are healed when the greater condition is taken care of.

We must always remember that our true role in healing is to bring the individual into a balanced attunement within himself, so that the God-force can give that which is needed at every level. This is no less true with regard to economic or material conditions than it is when physical ones are concerned. When the problems in the person's attitudes and relationships are faced and healed, then the economic and material conditions change.

## A Link in a Chain

In coming together as a group we must realize that each one brings certain strengths, certain weaknesses. It is in working together toward the ideal and purpose of being of service to others that we are the most effective. However, each has a work to do within self and for the good of the whole.

... each may present their bodies a living sacrifice, which is a reasonable service. To some there has been given the ability to serve as prophets; some as teachers; some as ministers; some in one manner, some in another; which are spiritual gifts, and of the same source, when applied in that manner that brings service to the fellow man; for in sending the Son into the world, as flesh, becoming the Son of man, man's service to God becomes then fellow service to fellow man, and through same exemplifying God's gift to the world.                  254-31

The blessings of the fathers rest upon the labors of those who would serve—serve—serve.                  254-18

We should each have this prayer and attitude:

God make me worthy to enter into the Holy of Holies and understand how I may serve my fellow man in giving the essence of life to many.                  254-20

We must continually be aware that the ego rears its ugly head within us, claiming for *self* that which has been accomplished through the group by the Spirit.

... let each—each—know themselves [to be] a link in the chain, as a spoke in the wheel. Do not [try to] be the whole, but fulfill that *thou* may do, that there may be the perfect accord; for he that giveth a cup of water in His name is greater than he that conquereth a city for his own aggrandizement.   262-20

The group forges links of light and love as its members work together, binding themselves together at the level of mind and spirit, enabling the group, through His Spirit, to accomplish miracles. During a healing meditation at the Week of Attunement on August 20, 1972, one man attending had this experience:

"I saw a chain link of light around each one of the 17 channels who were doing the laying on of hands. Each link was joined to the other and there was something written on each link. As I looked more closely, I could see the word LOVE written on each link."

This was, of course, a subjective individual experience; however, in the minds and hearts of all those who attended there was experienced the bonds of love, hope, and faith that can come only when the Spirit is truly present. These are the bonds which each group must strive to forge so that it may be as effective as it should be.

## *Work with a Prayer List*

In order that the work we are about may proceed in decency and order, it becomes necessary very quickly for each group to have its own prayer list. We need to pray regularly, daily, for those who are requesting prayer through our group. Even the Glad Helpers Prayer Group, which is responsible for the monthly A.R.E. international prayer list of more than 250 names of people for whom we pray daily, has its own local list of individuals for whom we also pray. One cannot hold all of these names in mind; therefore it is good and helpful to have them written down so that they may be individually focused upon. This list should be reviewed monthly, with the names of people who have been healed or who do not continue to seek prayer help being removed.

Frequently those who request prayer think that this is as far as their own responsibility goes. They sometimes have an attitude of, "Okay now, let's see what God and your group can do for me." But people seeking help through prayer need to have an attitude of expectancy, knowing that they can be helped, and of cooperation, willingness on their part to keep a regular prayer and meditation time so that they may be receptive to the creative force working within them. He who expects little will not be disappointed, while he who expects much may receive a miracle.

On our part, there needs to be the realization that as we help to heal others, we ourselves are healed. This would be recognized if we understood that it is the living Spirit within us that does the healing and which is sent out to others. This in turn stimulates the creative healing force within them, begins healing the body-mind-soul of each one, and flows out to others. Whatever a person gives out always comes back to him.

Whether we are working individually or in a group, we continue to be concerned about the most effective way we can pray for others. This question came up in 1932:

**Q-8. Should we hold each individual name separately in meditation, or hold the list as a group?**

**A-8.** This may be done either way, but it should be done in unison for the better effect. This may be alternated from time to time, even as He did. As He gave, "As ye have seen me do, do ye likewise, and greater things than I have done ye may do in my name, for I go to the Father." 281-5

The Glad Helpers Prayer Group worked with this advice for years, concluding from their experience that their work could be carried out most effectively through daily prayer for each person individually, by name. To me the name is the address of the soul; each name has its own vibratory pattern. The energy, when directed by thought to the person of that name, is drawn to its source; hence the necessity for using the whole name when praying aloud in a group. When we use a name, such as Mary, in our silent prayers, we have one specific person in mind, and the energy goes to that one because of our thought. However, when we say "Mary" aloud in a group, each member thinks of a different Mary or many different individuals by that name, and the energy is splayed in all directions.

There is a name to each soul . . . the name is relative to that which is accomplished by the soul in its sojourn throughout its whole experience . . . and in the end the name is the sum total of what the soul-entity in all of its vibratory forces has borne toward the Creative Force itself. 281-30

Many say, "Oh, God knows the names of all those we're praying for, so it isn't necessary for us to identify each person for Him by name." Of course, that is true; but it is we who are entrusted with working for Him in the earth. We are the custodians of our part of the Spirit, and we need to be used by it as effectively as we know how. Just consider: If *you* asked someone to pray for you and he said "Yes" and then lumped you with dozens of other names and prayed for you and the others "as a group"—how would you feel? Do you think that prayer would be as beneficial for *you* as it would be if you were being prayed for by name? The rule still holds: "Do unto others . . ."

There were a number of specific questions asked about working with and cooperating with those who had requested to be on the prayer list. These may be found in reading 281-8, questions and answers 1 through 8, published in *Meditation,* Part I, which is Volume 2 of the A.R.E. Library Series.

The question of whether to pray aloud or silently within the group is sometimes raised. Edgar Cayce was asked this question:

*Q-8. . . . If the spoken word is stronger than thought, why is it I prefer to use the silent meditation?*

**A-8.** In each, as has been given in vibration, there is the *sounding,* as it were, of those elements as manifest of the spirit in the material activity in each individual. So in self, no fault may be found that this becomes a higher vibration to self than were the word spoken. Neither does it change the fact that to the more individuals it is true that the spoken word makes a higher vibration. Just the condition or attunement of self. Don't find fault, or try to be like someone else—or try to have someone else be like you. Be like Him—all of you!　　　281-9

I have been in groups in which certain individuals were terribly upset when other members offered verbal prayers which they considered too long or indications of an "ego trip." Many others are uncomfortable praying aloud. There is a place for both silent prayer and verbal prayer. When a person is "tuned in," his prayer can lift a group right into the presence of God. Such experiences come to be valued and sought for; the soul longs for companionship with others and with Him, and it finds that fulfillment at such times.

All of us have heard and laughed at the quip made by the minister who, when he was asked to pray louder at a dinner meeting, said: "I'm not talking to you, I'm talking to God." If someone is "talking to God," then it surely should be done in *silence;* if he is seeking to raise the consciousness of the group to an awareness of their relationship to Him, of their gratitude for the abundance of all of life, then that prayer should be loud enough for everyone to hear. And so, the cardinal rule should always be: When praying aloud, pray loud enough for others to hear, so that they may be raised and quickened by your prayer.

### Format for the Group

We have discussed processes and procedures that can be used within a prayer group, so at this point I would like to share with you the format of the Glad Helpers Prayer-Healing Group.

### GLAD HELPERS PRAYER-HEALING GROUP

Meeting Time: Wednesday, 9:30 A.M.—12:00 N.
Usual Procedure:
Any significant modifications are to be discussed with the group in advance.
  I. Moment of silence.
 II. Scripture for the day, during which the head-and-neck and breathing exercises may be used.
III. Chanting.
IV. Short prayers of attunement offered by any who wish.
 V. Lord's Prayer.

VI. Affirmation: Use the affirmation of the month sent out with the monthly prayer list (always at the top of the first page).

VII. Meditation.

VIII. Calling of the names on the monthly prayer list:

Names are called from the prayer list by members of the group whose names have been drawn. Five chairs are used to represent the four prayer periods and the list of those who have passed on, which is called by the Prayer Secretary, Ruth LeNoir.

As the healing power is raised in each of us, let us direct it to the channels chosen.

IX. Prayers offered, silently or aloud, for any others who have requested prayer.

X. Surrounding prayers of protection are offered, silently or aloud, for those about whom we are concerned, but who have not requested prayer.

XI. Prayers for ourselves and for those to the right and the left of us.

XII. Prayers for the world and for our nation.

XIII. Laying on of hands:

We have a number of chairs in the middle of the circle, facing east. Members of the group who have worked with cleansing and preparing themselves to be channels may put their names into a basket; from this basket are then drawn enough names of people to stand behind all the chairs except one or two. One or two chairs are "left open" so that anyone present may ask another who has indicated his interest and preparedness to do the laying on of hands for him.

Anyone may "sit in" for absentee healing for someone else, provided that person has asked him to do so.

XIV. Prayers of thanksgiving.

Possible benediction: "May the Lord bless you and keep you. May the Lord make His face to shine upon you, and be gracious to you. May the Lord lift up His countenance upon you, and give you peace."   Numbers 6:24-26

XV. Continued study of the material: Prayer Group readings, 281 Series (published as *Meditation,* Part I, in the A.R.E. Library Series).

XVI. Business meeting:

Prayer requests.

Reading of any letters.

Reports on pertinent subjects: healing, meetings, etc.

XVII. Close with the 23rd Psalm. Stand in a circle holding hands, with the left palm up and the right palm down, to pass the energy.

71

*Prayer List:*
Anyone, anywhere, may put his own name on the prayer list. To do this, give your complete name and address and the time you keep for prayer and meditation to Ruth LeNoir, Prayer Group Secretary, or to any other member of the group.

It has been suggested in the readings that you should keep the same time each day for prayer and meditation and that in seeking for healing for yourself you should pray for yourself and others who are seeking healing. Indeed, in healing others we are healed ourselves. Each one who seeks is encouraged to pray for himself and for all others who are on the list at the same time.

*Growth in the Spiritual Life:*
We strongly encourage each participant in the Prayer-Healing Group to begin or to continue his activity in a Search for God Group and/or in his Church as a way of systematic spiritual growth and development.

It has been suggested that each month the chairman of the healing group invite any member who is not active in a Search for God group to become active.

*History of the Group:*
The group and the readings for them began as a result of a dream Edgar Cayce had the night that he gave the first Search for God reading, in September, 1931. A "most important part of the work" had been omitted and so was begun and has continued as a part of the Search for God program.

*Suggested Reading:*
The Bible
*Prayer Group Readings* (including readings on the Revelation), 281 Series; now available as *Meditation,* Part I (Vol. 2 of the A.R.E. Library Series)

*Meditation,* Part II (Vol. 3 of the A.R.E. Library Series)

*Meditation and the Mind of Man,* by Dr. Herbert B. Puryear and Mark Thurston

Circulating file on *Meditation* from the Edgar Cayce readings

*Gifts of Healing,* by Hugh Lynn Cayce

*That Ye May Heal,* by Mary Ann Woodward

"A Philosophy of Healing," *The A.R.E. Journal,* Vol. VI, No. 5, Sept., 1971, by Meredith Ann Puryear

Becoming a part of a prayer-healing group brings with it the responsibility of living, acting, and giving that which is known to be in accord with truth.

As to the activities of the group, there has been that which should cause in the experience of each more and more the consciousness of the truth in the crucified Christ manifesting in the lives, the experience of others, and that—as He has given—"Ye that seek in My name, believing and acting and keeping those commandments which I have given thee, shall ask and receive" . . .

As to that which may be given respecting healing through prayer, meditation, and the *sending out to others* of that which is raised in the consciousness of those that seek through the promises in Him to be a blessing, an aid, to their fellow man: He has given, and it has been accorded by those that came after to declare those things that had been proclaimed in the activities in the earth, that those who would first consecrate their own lives to the service of their fellow man could—and would, through concerted activity in prayer, meditation—bring in the experience of others that sought by them in earnestness and in truth, that they might through such aid, such counsel, such an activity, know in their own selves the glory of those promises made in Him.

Then, as ye in thy activities come seeking for thy own brother who asks that ye remember him, that ye aid him, do so in that manner He, the Master, has set forth: "As ye seek in my name, believing, ye shall receive in thine experience." [author's italics]                                              281-21

In bringing this chapter on prayer-group work to a close, I should like to conclude even as did this reading:

In giving counsel to those of the prayer group:
Let each seek more and more, in their daily lives, to be one of those sent by the Lord, the Christ, to someone, to awaken them to their opportunities in the love of the Christ.

Then, let each of you so act yourself that those to whom ye speak *know* ye walk and talk often with the Lord, with the Christ.

For He hath chosen each of you as a messenger to someone. Fail Him not.                                              281-64

# Chapter Six
# ATTITUDES AND EMOTIONS
### The First Step That Leads to Illness or Health

*Introduction*

That which we continually dwell upon in thought, coupled with what we eat, is what we become at the physical-flesh level. When we dwell upon negativity, jealousy, anger, fear, selfishness, and/or hate, we literally bring death, destruction, and decay to our own bodies and poison the atmosphere around us. Conversely, when we dwell in joy, happiness, forgiveness, considerateness, understanding, patience, and love, we bring health to our own bodies and draw light to the earth so that those about us are uplifted.

We have discussed the principle of Oneness from varied angles. It is hard for us to be monists, because our lives are so fragmented and our minds so divided. We need to realize that—though the body-mind-soul can be thought of as three separate structures when theorizing, in order to come to a better understanding of each—in reality these structures form a whole, a single unit which makes up one entity. Nothing goes on at one level that does not affect the others.

What I eat over a period of time leads to a pattern of either health or illness, and thus either enhances or upsets the flow of the life force in my body. What I think and dwell upon continually leads to either life or death, helping or hindering the body in its desire for health and wholeness. When I feed my soul with prayer, meditation, life- and light-giving Scriptures, and communion with God, the flow of the Spirit through the body and the mind animates the whole; when these spiritual nutrients are lacking, the body and mind are literally starved of the Breath of Life.

There is so much in the readings of Edgar Cayce that helps us to understand all of life, to get a clearer picture of what we as entities are about in the earth, and to perceive more clearly the greatness that has been and is still being manifested through the work of Jesus Christ. By far the majority of the readings that Mr. Cayce gave were sought because of physical conditions. It is from these that we learn how greatly the mind, the attitudes that we hold, affects the mental and physical conditions of the body. I sincerely believe that as we come to understand the relationship among the three aspects of body-mind-spirit we will grow in our desire to change our destructive attitudes.

Let us now examine a large portion of one physical reading so that we may see how one area of our being impinges upon the others. Please note that the original suggestion asks for the *cause* of the existing conditions, and observe how Mr. Cayce ties in the mental-spiritual orientation and the resultant physical condition with basic spiritual laws.

### READING

*Mrs. Cayce: You will go over this body carefully, examine it thoroughly, and tell me the conditions you find at the present time; giving the* cause *of the existing conditions, also suggestions for help and relief of this body; answering the questions, as I ask them:*

Mr. Cayce: Yes, we have the body here, [3078].[7]

In giving that as may be helpful for this body, we find that many things must be taken into consideration.

While there is the attempt at times for the entity or body to seek spiritual influences, these—spiritual forces—those tenets and truths—are not merely as laws or cloaks that may be put on and taken off.

For, as indicated, there are physical disturbances in the body. To be sure, these may be healed by divine forces. But, as given by Him who is the law, who is the healer of *all* disease, "He that saith he loveth the Lord and hateth his brother is a liar and the truth is not in him."

He that loveth not then the ways of the Lord—not merely as applied to self but as self may apply to those the body meets day by day—need not expect the law of grace to be effective in his experience. Ye cannot hate, or doubt, or fear those things about self, or those things that would be used by others, and expect the law of love to be effective in thee. For, the condemnation of self in others falls on self! And, as the entity will and does find, as the psalmist gave, "That which I hated has come upon me."

Then there is little need for attempting to heal an ill body unless the mind, the purpose, the ideal of the entity is set in Him

---

7. To preserve privacy, names used in the readings were subsequently replaced with numbers. Each series of readings given for a specific person or about a particular topic was assigned a separate number.

who is peace, life, hope and understanding. For He is indeed the way and the truth and the light.

If the entity will apply in self that it *knows* to do—not as something that applies to self alone, but that applies to self in its relationships to others—the results will be apparent. Ye *apply* thy love, if ye would have others love thee! Ye do trust others and ye *are* the trust and the hope, if ye would have hope or expect others to have hope and trust in thee!

For as ye know, as ye interpret in thine own experience, as in the life of Him who—though without fault—was hated of others. "If the world hate me, it does and it will hate thee." But if ye hate the world, if ye dislike those with whom ye are associated, then *His* death, His love, His promise becomes of none effect in thee!

For the *world* hath hated Him without a cause. Ye feel within thyself that ye are distrusted, that ye are hated without a cause. But if ye do the same in return, His promise becomes of none effect in thee—ye are of the world and not of Him.

In thy body—ye find body, mind, soul; or the spiritual, mental and material body. The misapplication of truth in thy mind, in not interpreting the spirit in self, may—as in thine own experience—bring the lack of proper elimination of drosses from thy body.

It is true that ye may in the spiritual, in the mental, in the material, make applications of that cleansing that may aid the body in eliminating same from the physical, from the mental, from the spiritual. The spirit is ever willing, and it remains the same yesterday, today and forever. For it is the eternal spiritual law.

First, then, the mental attitude towards self, towards the world, towards others, must be changed. For, if ye recognize in self the truth, that which is and was manifested in the Christ Consciousness, ye will change thy mental attitude—towards self, towards others, towards conditions about thee. *Then* ye may see change in the physical results or manifestations in self. Then ye, too, as He gave of old, will wash and be clean every whit!                                          3078-1

We see in this reading the hard question that was always directed to a person seeking physical healing: Why do you want to be healed? What are you going to do with health once you achieve it? Are you going to use your body for selfishness, self-centeredness, or do you have some purpose of service? We have this poignant statement from this reading: " . . . there is little need for attempting to heal an ill body unless the mind, the purpose, the ideal of the entity is set in Him who is peace, life, hope and understanding." (3078-1) Why is there little need for attempting to heal the body unless the other conditions are met? Because frequently the physical body simply manifests the symptoms of a sick soul.

I hasten to say "frequently" because illness has many causes, including the attitudinal one. It is important to emphasize at this point that this material is included so that one may use it for *self-examination* and not for judgment of others. Let us not become "Job's comforters" with our knowledge, readily pointing out to others their negative attitudes and the resultant conditions. On the other hand, if with gentleness of insight we can help ourselves and others look more closely at attitudes, we may be able to speed healing and recovery.

### Attitudes Toward Self and Others That Affect the Body

Remember, the mental attitudes will have much to do with whether you will grow a straight toenail or keep your eyes straight, or keep your voice when you are upset. For these work with the glands of the sensory system.

... Remember that the attitude of mind has much to do with the conditions of the body—this body particularly.     3376-1

*Anger:*

These should be warnings for *every* human: Madness is certainly poison to the system.     2-14

Anger may bring heart and/or liver trouble, because as poisons are produced within the system the liver is unable to flush them out.

*Neglect:*

Negligence is as much a sin as anything else. Somehow we have glorified the wife, mother, doctor, or social worker who neglects her or his own health and well-being to care for others. However, just think how much more effective one might be in service, and for how much greater a length of time, if one truly cared for his own body. Neglect is linked to the sin of omission. When we omit getting enough rest, eating the right foods, and praying and meditating, we rob ourselves of those things that will bring us length of days, strength of body, and firmness of direction.

... first the service is to self or in self, that there is made a better flow of the coordinating activities of life and vitality in itself; thus better fitting the body for a service to the patient and to those of mankind in general.     1216-1

When we take time to rest, play, pray, meditate, and eat correctly, we literally re-create our bodies. This is good preventive therapy, just as massage and regular osteopathic or chiropractic adjustments help keep the body in good tone and alignment so that it will not become ill.

*Hate:*

That which we hate or fear we draw to ourselves. The Scriptures put it this way: "For the thing that I fear comes upon me . . . " (Job 3:25) This concept and related ones are expressed frequently in the Cayce readings:

And let not thine condemnation bring upon thee that ye hate. For that ye hate ye become. This is the law.               1261-1

Do not belittle, do not hate. For hate *creates,* as does love— and brings turmoils and strifes.               1537-1

. . . "He that hateth his brother has committed as great a sin as he that slayeth a man," for the deed is as of an accomplishment in the mental being, which is the builder for every entity.               243-10

No one can hate his neighbor and not have stomach or liver trouble.               4021-1

. . . here we find that hate and animosity and anxiety may be the poison that causes *much* of the disturbance [prostatitis].
*Live* more in keeping with that as thou hast professed . . . Did He justify Himself before His accusers? Did He attempt to even meet the words that were spoken condemning Him? 1196-11

*Jealousy:*

. . . self-indulgences . . . next to jealousy, sap the spiritual purpose in the mental attributes of body and mind of an individual manifested in materiality.               2390-7

No one can be jealous and allow the anger of same and not have upset digestion or heart disorder.               4021-1

Yes—as we find, conditions are not good here. Much of these may be aided, but unless there is the change in the approach to healing, what will be the application of same?
All healing comes from the divine within, that is creative. Thus, if one would correct physical or mental disturbances, it is necessary to change the attitude and to let the life forces become constructive and not destructive. Hate, malice and

jealousy only creates poisons within the minds, souls and
bodies of people.                                          3312-1

*Judgment:*

   ...judge not too harshly thyself nor others—remembering, it
is with the measure ye mete to others that it is measured to
thee again.                                                1793-2

*Resentment and Grudges:*

   Just as these attitudes eat away at your mental being, if they
are held onto long enough they may result in a cancer that
literally eats away at your body. Some possible "minor" effects
of resentment are inflammation, hives, circulatory difficulties,
and pancreas trouble.

   And keep the constructive mental attitude. Never
resentments, for this naturally creates within the system
those secretions that are hard upon any circulation, and
especially where there is disturbance with the spleen, the
pancreas and a portion of the liver activity.              470-19

   ...less of animosities, less of holding grudges or those things
which make the entity speak of others unkindly ... these
destructive attitudes bring on self all the pent up feelings and
they find expression in irritations [hives].               5226-1

   One may not pray with long prayers of thankfulness for this
or that, as in the experience of others, and still hold a grudge or
a feeling of animosity, or a feeling of undue consideration for
other individuals at least attempting—in their own ways—to
be of help, whether in a feeble way or in whatever way. For all
power that is in the hands of man has been *lent,* and it is not of
man's knowledge but of God.
   Thus when individuals hold a grudge they are fighting the
God within themselves against the God within the individual
or soul for whom or towards whom such is held.             1304-1

   In the fall of 1968, when we were living in San Antonio,
Texas, I was working in a Presbyterian prayer group and with
our A.R.E. Prayer Group. Three people came to me asking for
the special prayers of our groups and requesting help in
understanding what was happening with family members who
had been diagnosed as terminal cancer patients with only a
short while to live. In each case I suggested talking frankly
with the person, asking him to examine his attitudes of
resentment and to pray for help in letting go of them at the

same time we were praying for him. In each case this was done, and within a three-month period each family member had a sudden "spontaneous remission."

*Fear:*

... for being afraid is the first consciousness of sin's entering in, for he that is made afraid has lost consciousness of self's own heritage with the Son; for we are heirs through Him to that kingdom that is beyond all of that that would make afraid, or that would cause a doubt in the heart of any. Through the recesses of the heart, then, search out that that would make afraid, casting out fear, and *He* alone may guide.     243-10

Fear is the root of most of the ills of mankind, whether of self, or of what others think of self, or what self will appear to others. To overcome fear is to fill the mental, spiritual being, with that which wholly casts out fear; that is, as the love that is manifest in the world through Him who gave Himself the ransom for many. Such love, such faith, such understanding, casts out fear. Be ye not fearful; for that thou sowest, that thou must reap. Be more mindful of that sown!     5459-3

*Condemnation of Self and Others:*

Then to *condemn* self, in the activity towards others, is to *build* that which is destructive.     1439-1

The entity then was the minister, or the associate minister, who caused the uprising and the condemnation of children who saw, who heard, who experienced the voices of those in the inter-between . . .
Hence the entity physically has experienced the ducking, from its own self, in its daily activities [enuresis—bedwetting]...     2779-1

### What We Don't Use We Lose

There seems to be a general law that "what we don't use, we lose." That is, if there is a physical faculty which we possess and we do not work with it constructively, then we are in danger of losing it. Do you ever wonder why America is such a land of people who wear glasses? Have we lost the ability to *see* conditions around us that need our attention?

I recently worked with a young woman who came to the Prayer Group seeking the laying on of hands because she was going blind in one eye. After working with her for some time, it became apparent that her condition was caused by her inability to "look at" a situation of dis-ease between herself and

80

her children. Once she began to work with that, her eye began to improve greatly. A man who came for help, complaining that he was rapidly becoming deaf, had a "miraculous" recovery when he was asked to consider prayerfully the condition in his life relationships to which he had become deaf.

Give, then, in broader fields of activity, in *every* channel where those that are seeking may find; that are wandering, that are lame in body, lame in mind, halt in their manner of expression, that are blind to the beauties in their own household, their own hearts, their own minds. These thou may awaken in all thy fields. And as ye do, greater is thy vision—and He will guide thee, for He hath given His angels charge concerning those that seek to be a channel of blessing to their fellow man; that purge their hearts, their bodies, of every selfish motive and give the Christ—*crucified, glorified*—a place in its stead.                                  696-3

### Conditions to Be Worked With in Attitude

*Epilepsy:*

Here we have conditions, then, that are prenatal that are causing the seizures that are a part of the experience of this entity.

These can be relieved. It will almost require the training of the body mentally to rely upon the divine within.

Here we find the better association would be with a nurse or a constant companion, almost all the while—or in regular periods, at least; one such as a student of Unity or Christian Science.

You see, these groups have something on the Church—that the Church has left out ordinarily. They trust in the divinity of the Christ wholly set as a central theme of the mind.

This is needed in this particular entity individually, so that the personality and the mental self may take on not the extremes in either but the universality of the Christ Consciousness in the individuality and personality of this entity.                                  3430-1

*Eliminations:*

The misapplication of truth in thy mind, in not interpreting the spirit in self, may—as in thine own experience—bring the lack of proper elimination of drosses from thy body.  3078-1

*Paralysis:*

The same with individuals where there is in their experience crosses to bear, hardships or surroundings that to them are overpowering, overwhelming, by slights, slurs, and fancies of the inactivity of a coordinating force. If these are held continually as crosses, or as things to be overcome, they will remain as crosses. But if they are to be met with the spirit of truth and right in their own selves, they should create *joy;* for that is what will be built.                                    552-2

## Asthmatic Condition:

For if each soul would learn not to make itself anxious, it would be able to control the mental, and when controlling the mental we control the environs of the body.         3127-2

## Muscular Dystrophy:

**Q-1. What causes her malady (diagnosed first as multiple sclerosis) [lastly as progressive muscular dystrophy]?**
A-1. These conditions are karmic as well as a general physical disability through chemical changes in the body, and the inability to reproduce itself.

One should consider, as in this body, that the physical body in its creation was and is given the ability to reproduce itself. Thus each organ, each portion of the body secretes, from the physical, the mental and the spiritual life, that needed to reproduce itself for a growth to better conditions—or the realm for which it prepares itself. When these activities break down, these have to be supplied or they call on other portions of the organism—and thus they become overcharged or undernourished. Then disintegration begins in one form or another.                                    3337-1

## Hardheartedness:

Live with this in mind (and every soul take heed): *Ye shall pay every whit, that ye break the law of the Lord.* For the law of the Lord is perfect, it converteth the soul. It doesn't always convert a hardhearted man nor a body that is beset with habits that have left their mark upon those portions of the body through which soul and mind may work. What are these?

Nerve and blood forces of the body! The heart, that is the engine of the body itself.                                    3559-1

## Conclusion

The pessimism and despair of those about us has brought and will continue to bring disintegration and destructive forces to our world and within our society. Balance and harmony will be brought into being only as those of us who know in whom we believe and realize that He is able to keep that which we have committed unto Him live the life of enlightened understanding and love. Any who read the following words must realize that there is a great work of healing to be accomplished within ourselves and within our society.

... above all, *pray!* Those who are about the body, use, rely upon the spiritual forces. For the prayer of the righteous shall save the sick.

Know that all strength, all healing of every nature is the changing of the vibrations from within—the attuning of the divine within the living tissue of a body to Creative Energies. This alone is healing. Whether it is accomplished by the use of drugs, the knife or whatnot, it is the attuning of the atomic structure of the living cellular force to its spiritual heritage.

Then, in the prayer of those—live day by day in the same manner as ye pray—if ye would bring assistance and help for this body.                                                    1967-1

Would that all men would know, much more may be accomplished through the prayer of those that truly make of themselves one with the Creative Forces that have been manifested in the earth through Him that gave Himself that men might have the access to the Father, than through all the power and might of men. Though the worlds shall pass away, His word shall *not* pass away.                              731-1

# Chapter Seven
# HEALING THROUGH THE LAYING ON OF HANDS

There are many methods of spiritual healing; it can be brought about by a word, a look, or a touch. We would say that all healing is ultimately spiritual, though it may be stimulated by drugs, surgery, massage, or manipulation. No one method is necessarily holier than any other. We have each built our own consciousness through time, and each of us is totally unique; therefore, it takes different things to awaken the healing force within the bodies of different people. We should learn to be accepting of ourselves, understanding our own strengths and weaknesses. We must learn through time and patience that the body is so designed that, because of its very nature—because of the *élan vital,* the God-force resident within it—it will heal itself when we stimulate that force with whatever is compatible to it.

There may be times when one needs medication and other times when perfect well-being may be achieved through prayer or the laying on of hands. We should endeavor to become so attuned in our awareness of our bodies that we will know when to see a doctor, when to take an aspirin, and when prayer will be sufficient. I know that the more consistent I am with my meditation and prayer periods, the healthier I am, and the more quickly I am able to bring about almost instantaneous healing of burns, headaches, and other conditions within my own body.

I know that many who work with spiritual healing say it is impossible to heal oneself or a loved one. There is no basis in spiritual law for this viewpoint. If it is true that we can raise in another only that which we have been able to bring about within ourselves (and I know that it is), then unless we are able to bring some measure of wholeness to ourselves—or rather, unless we are able to become so attuned that the God-force can do this—then we have little to give to another in the manner of spiritual healing.

Paul says there are many gifts, but only one Spirit (I Cor. 12). As a friend of mine, a minister, said of me, my "thing"—or my developing awareness—seems to be working with the laying on of hands. In seeking to share in this way, I find that I can tell a great deal about a person and sometimes am able to give special help; there are many in our Prayer Group and around the nation who also find themselves with a growing sensitivity in this area. It is a gift that can be developed more fully through desire, dedication, and application.

As we grow in the spiritual life, in nearness to God, and in love toward our fellow man, in some there is awakened a desire to be of help and service in this particular manner. Generally the interest is present long before an opportunity for formal application is presented. I say "formal" because we all have dozens of informal opportunities daily to direct healing by thought to those whom we touch. We don't require dim lights and a holy setting, nor must those to whom healing is directed be informed that we are going to do laying on hands for them.

One of the most awkward and difficult situations in which I have ever found myself came about when a well-meaning friend took me to the hospital room of a total stranger. The woman pronounced to the patient, "Now you're going to have the laying on of hands." The patient was obviously apprehensive, dubious, and uncomfortable, just as I was. If the person had simply introduced me as a friend, I know I could have worked with prayer and a light touch and been much more effective and helpful. As it was, we had a very stiff and, to my mind, unfruitful period together. It is still painful for me to recall.

In sharp contrast to this episode, there have been many occasions when the patient knew of my interest and work with healing and requested my presence; with the patient's cooperation, we were able to bring him close to the Divine Presence, where healing was invited, accepted, and manifested. Much more frequent still are those occasions on which I meet to talk with a friend or acquaintance, begin to be aware of his distress at one level or another, and simply reach out to touch him, sending a silent blessing and sensing an instantaneous response.

The laying on of hands has long been shrouded in mystery, as has all faith healing. Just as we have tried to remove prayer from the land of the pious, so, too, would we like to take the gift of touch into the realm of everyday living. Everyone is familiar with the healing that a mother can bring to a child merely by touching him; when she gathers that child into her arms, her whole body exudes love and healing. As you think about those you know and love, and about others you are acquainted with, you could probably easily group them into at least three categories: (1) those whose touch is "good"; (2) those whom you would rather not touch you; and (3) those whom you *don't mind* touching you, but whom you would not *seek* to touch you.

It seems, obviously, that the first step in developing the ability to heal through touch is to become the kind of person that others want to be near, the kind to whom they are drawn. When there is the entering into one's closet in close communion with God, it will not need to be advertised; others will know intuitively and seek you out. Proclaiming "I am a healer" is the surest way I know to make people apprehensive. Indeed, it is almost a cardinal rule never to ask others to let you do the laying on of hands for them; unless they seek you out they are not ready for what God may have to give them through you. The more we focus on others and their needs, the less we need to be concerned about our own shortcomings; when we provide the channel and they are open to receive, there is no limit to what the Spirit can do.

One woman who asked Edgar Cayce if she was able to heal through the laying on of hands was told, "This may be developed in self, even as the vibrations may be raised in self and in others. When there is that impelling force that arises to *do,* by word *or* by act, or by that raising in self, ACT in *that* direction and manner." (281-10) I think it important to note that she was told to act when there was that impelling force from within to do so. That urge to act may come anywhere—in a home, a park, a lecture, a store; and it can arise any time you touch—or even just share a compassionate glance with—a friend, a child, or a stranger.

One of the phrases used in the above quotation is "even as the vibrations may be raised in self and in others." This raising of the vibrations within self, or making the attunement within self, is so germane to healing of every nature that we may too quickly take it for granted that everyone understands and appreciates this process.

The more one works with the tools of meditation and prayer—through time and in patience coming to understand that the very nature of our being is spiritual, our heritage is that of children of God, and the destiny of every soul is in Him—the more easily one is able at any time to raise the consciousness (vibrations) to the Divine within self and thus within others. Within the body, the energy is propelled upward from the gonads, goes through the lyden to the pineal, and spills over into the pituitary, from which it may be directed outward like a ray. Part of the energy flows back down through the body for the cleansing, purifying, and healing of the self, and it may flow out through the hands when the directing thought so urges. With time and practice, it becomes as easy to do this informally, outside meditation, as it is formally, within the meditation period.

As the body attunes self, as has been given, it may be a channel where there may be even *instant* healing with the laying on of hands. The more often this occurs the more *power* is there felt in the body, the more forcefulness in the act or word. 281-5

This statement indicates that the potential exists and that the ability will grow with application. For some strange reason we choose to remain very naive about the gifts of the Spirit. Unless they come full-blown, we remain skeptical. Yet everything in life teaches us that the more we do anything, the more skill we develop in it. From the moment of birth we have to *learn* to walk, talk, care for ourselves, play, and develop skills, ad infinitum. Surely, then, we need an awareness of the potential that may be developed in a variety of ways relating to the spiritual life.

*Q-21. . . . Could I become a healer? If so, what method should I use?*
A-21. That as seemeth to thee that channel through which an individual, or entity, may get hold of that which is being given out by self. There are, as seen, many *various* channels through which healing may come. That as of the individual contact; that as of the faith; that as of the laying on of hands; that as will create in the mind (for it is the builder in a human being) that consciousness that makes for the closer contact with the universal, or the *Creative* Forces, in its experience. That which is nearest akin to that concept built. Use that thou hast, then, in hand. 281-6

When we are truly interested in helping others, we must not become hung up in the method we will use to achieve that end. We must limit neither ourselves and the way God may work through us nor the person that we may help. We need to be sufficiently open to the movement of the Spirit that we may reach out to the other's consciousness and give that which is required. And as we can give only that which we have "in hand," we need to develop an ever broader base from which to minister.

When a body, separate from that one ill, then, has so attuned or raised its own vibrations sufficiently, it may—by the motion of the spoken word—awaken the activity of the emotions to such an extent as to revivify, resuscitate or to change the rotary force or influence or the atomic forces in the activity of the structural portion, or the *vital* forces of a body, in such a way and manner as to set it again in motion.

Thus does spiritual or psychic influence of body upon body bring healing to any individual; where another body may raise that necessary influence in the hormone of the circulatory forces as to take from that within itself to revivify or resuscitate diseased, disordered or distressed conditions within a body.                                                    281-24

If these two paragraphs were punctuated differently, they would be somewhat easier to understand. I think the first half of the sentence beginning the second paragraph completes the thought of the first paragraph. The second half of that same sentence gives an entirely different method of spiritual healing. In the first method of spiritual healing, a person so raises the vibrations within himself that with the spoken word (or a touch, a glance, or whatnot) he is able to affect the vibratory pattern of the other person so as to change the rotary forces at the atomic level of the cell structure, bringing resuscitation or revivication of the perfect pattern. In the second type of healing described above, a person raises the hormone activity within his own body to the point where he is able to take from within himself that which is needed to rebuild or resuscitate diseased, disordered, or distressed portions of the other body.

I feel that we are only at the threshold of understanding what is involved in the two different methods of spiritual healing. The first form comes about as a result of attuning oneself to the Source, or becoming a channel through which there may be a flow of spiritual energy. The other method, designated elsewhere in the readings as magnetic healing, involves drawing the energy from within one's own bodily forces.

Nowhere in the Prayer Group readings, which were given to a *group* of people who were seeking to be of service to mankind, is working with magnetic healing recommended; rather, the encouragement was always to develop the attunement and become a channel through which God's energy may flow. In order to do this, one has to work with cleansing, healing, and purifying oneself. We are "recharged" with energy when working as a channel, not depleted. We may work with large numbers of people in this way.

By contrast, *individuals* were encouraged to work with magnetic healing on a one-to-one basis. They were told that they should be high in energy, as healing in this way would deplete them. The energy was described as "electrical," the method was called "hand therapy," and the flow could be started by rubbing the hands together vigorously. Those encouraged to use this method were relatives of the person in need of healing, or occasionally nurses, masseurs, or osteopaths who were close to the patient with whom they were working. They were told that it must be done prayerfully and in love, never when there was anger or hostility.

I believe that the case of the woman healed of an issue of

blood, as recounted in Mark 5:25-34, is an instance of magnetic healing. The woman reached out to touch Jesus' garments, and He perceived "that power had gone forth from Him ... " (Mark 5:30) In spiritual healing, one must have an opportunity to tune in, i.e., to get the spigot turned on, so that the Spirit may flow; in magnetic healing, one may dip from the well of his own reservoir, or another may "dip in" and there will be felt a draining away of energy.

In their article entitled "Your Color Aura" (*House and Garden,* September, 1975, p. 102), Thelma Moss and Kendall Johnson tell of using Kirlian photography to obtain pictures of the auras of healers working with patients. The authors report that the healthy auras of the healers were transferred to the patients, and the healers took on the depleted, "sick" auras of the patients. Such results suggest a process involving a magnetic treatment, with the vital energy of the healers being drained off, or given to the patients. When this is done without cleansing and purifying, there is the danger of the healer taking on the condition of the one he is trying to help.

In those individual readings in which the magnetic procedure was recommended, the focus was on the one to receive the "hand therapy," not on the one doing the application. On occasion it was suggested that more than one person make the application; however, in none of these readings was any such person referred to as a "healer." They were given a procedure that worked, that would be effective, and there frequently needed to be healing between the people involved in the magnetic treatment. It would have been very involved and complicated to get individuals who were interested in helping just one person get well, not mankind as a whole, to work on the entire process of spiritual healing.

Dolores Krieger, R.N., Ph.D., a professor of nursing at New York University, has begun working with a method of healing that involves the laying on of hands, and teaching it to both doctors and nurses. This method, which I would characterize as magnetic healing, has proved effective in bringing healing to many. We should not be surprised that, when there is the purpose of bringing help, the influence of a healthy body upon a an unhealthy one would allow the molecular structure of the diseased body to realign itself with the correct pattern. A force is drawn from (not through) one body and transmitted to another.

Ordinarily, when one speaks of magnetic healing he is concerned with simply a force field emanating from one body and acting upon and influencing another body; in such references there is generally no consideration of the ideal and no underlying understanding of the Creative Forces pervading the whole. Surely, any time doctors and nurses work with any healing method, they do so with the intention of bringing health to the patient, an explicit—if unstated—ideal. What is lacking is the broad-based understanding of the spiritual nature of all things; the danger here lies in having a too mechanistic view, one which cuts off the real breakthrough of growth in understanding.

**Q-7. Please explain the sensations during meditation of vibration running up through the body and ending in a sort of fullness in the head.**
**A-7. The various portions, as given, represent the activities that are being set, either when considered from the purely scientific or from the metaphysical standpoint, as an active force emanating from the Life itself within. Then, these become all-embracing; hence the better understanding should be gained, whether used to disseminate and bring healing or for the raising of the forces in self. *When one is able to so raise within themselves such vibrations, as to pass through the whole course of the attributes of the physical attunements, to the disseminating force or center, or the [third] eye,* then the body of that individual becomes a magnet that may (if properly used) bring healing to others with the laying on of hands. This is the manner in which such a healing becomes effective BY the laying on of hands. [author's italics]          281-14**

We see in this answer again the reference to the total attunement that can enable a person's body to become like a magnet through which healing vibrations can flow to another.

In the reading that follows, Mr. Cayce pointed out that those "afflicted in the imaginative system . . . " can be materially aided by the laying on of hands. I take this to mean that mental-emotional disturbances, as well as physical conditions, can be treated effectively in this way. Those who work with the laying on of hands do find that such conditions respond to this treatment.

*. . . there are some that are afflicted in the IMAGINATIVE system—as [146]. This will be materially aided by the laying on of hands of one that would aid in bringing help and aid to the body.* Others, as in [275]—as given—would be well that there be the laying on of hands, that there may be brought to each that physical CONSCIOUSNESS as brought about in their experience, or what is known or called by some karmic conditions—that may be overcome—they become, must become to the inner consciousness, and physical—and PHYSICAL activity, that may bring about an action through a form—or a removal of, as was necessary for the spittle and clay to heal the blind, or as was necessary in others, "Arise, take up thy bed and walk," or as to another, "Go show thyself

to the priest, conforming to the law thou art a part of!" Hence, in each there are those necessary things.

Do that. [author's italics]                                                    281-5

As the above reading also points out, another way of using the laying on of hands is to become so attuned to the one you are trying to help that you are able to tune in to karmic conditions that are affecting him and then bring these conditions to his consciousness. You can do this with verbal prayer, always exercising discretion and discernment. Whenever I am about to use this technique, I find myself praying for myself so that I may tune in to only that which will be helpful and so that I may then awaken the understanding of the other person and quicken his desire to work with whatever is given. It is often beneficial to suggest some appropriate activity to the person you are attempting to aid. Many times I pray that the individual will watch his dreams in order to gain further understanding and enlightenment, and at times I suggest that he take some particular action in relation to another person or a group.

... with the laying on of hands, that enables the individual, the entity so being aided, to have SOMETHING to hold on to that is as concrete as that it is battling with. Then, as is seen in the more CONCERTED action of the group, in their COOPERATIVE concerted action, and with the *continued* laying on of hands, there will come—as we find—a COMPLETE cure. [author's italics]                                281-5

Two valuable concepts are expressed in this statement. The first is that a spiritual activity that will help the person in his struggle to meet his problems at the physical and/or mentalemotional level needs to be incorporated into the life style. Through time, the laying on of hands can fill this role in our battle with our dragons. The second concept is that most healing does take time; seldom is there instantaneous healing, though it does occasionally occur. There is a rejuvenating, resuscitating activity that takes place over the weeks and months as one works with a weekly or a daily prayer period in which the laying on of hands is practiced.

The following excerpt suggests an affirmation to be used in meditation periods during which healing "magnetic powers..." are transmitted "from body to body . . . "

This should be given with those periods of meditation and the magnetic powers that go from body to body, as the superconsciousness and subconscious forces possess or direct the material or physical forces through the activity of the spiritual reactions in body:

The peace and the harmony that comes from the Father of light, and love, that is ours through the promises of the Christ in man, is possessing thy being—now—and making thee whole, as He would have thee—now!

In His name, in His power, be thou whole!          281-17

## Laying-on-of-Hands Healing Within the Church

The laying on of hands has a long tradition within the Judeo-Christian heritage. During the early part of this century, the most familiar and perhaps the only experience most American Christians had with the laying on of hands was in the ordination of ministers and, in some few denominations, when deacons and/or elders were installed in the Church; however, with the slow revival of healing within the Church by such movements as The Order of Saint Luke (of the Episcopal Church) and with the "popularization" of this practice by such notables as Oral Roberts and Kathryn Kuhlman, it lies now within the everyday awareness of most people.

Most clergymen have never been challenged by the concept of the priest-physician, either in their training or, it seems, in their reading of sacred Scripture. And yet, here, too, it seems that many are now being beckoned by a revival of interest and a renewed awareness of the challenge of the real spiritual life. Many ministers throughout the nation are allowing healing services to be conducted by lay people; i.e., when they become convinced of the reality of the working of the Spirit through someone else and yet find themselves lacking in this particular spiritual gift, in order to benefit the larger community they allow healing services with the laying on of hands to be held in their sanctuaries.

There is the feeling within many that what happens in the laying on of hands lies in the realm of hoax, magnetism, hypnotism, or magic; and, indeed, it may, depending upon the person who is practicing it and/or the situation in which it is performed. One must always use discernment, not prejudice, when evaluating anything. In being faced with the question of the validity of these occurrences, we are in a position similar to that of the Sadducees and Pharisees of Jesus' day, many of whom felt that His healings were hoaxes or the work of the devil. The proper criterion in such matters is ever the same—then as now: " . . . by their fruits ye shall know them." (Matt. 7:20, KJV) Does the experience bring healing at any level? Does it bring a renewed sense of hope, purpose, and relation to the Source of all life? Or does it bring discouragement, disappointment, unhappiness, and bitterness?

## Biblical References to the Laying on of Hands

*OLD TESTAMENT*

Deuteronomy 34:9
I Kings        17:17-24 Elijah using his whole body to raise a child from the dead
II Kings       4:14-37 Elisha using his whole body to raise a child from the dead

*NEW TESTAMENT*

### Parallel References

| Matthew: | | Mark: | | Luke: | |
|----------|---------|-------|---------|-------|---------|
| 8:2-3 | | 1:40-42 | | 5:12-13 | |
| 9:18-26 | | 5:21-43 | | 8:41-56 | |
| 19:13-15 | | 10:13-16 | | 18:15-17 | |

Mark:        6:5
             7:31-36
             8:22-26
             16:15-18

Luke:        4:40-41
             13:10-14

Acts:        8:14-17
             9:10-18
             13:1-3
             19:1-7
             19:11-12
             28:8-9

I Timothy:   4:14

II Timothy:  1:6

Hebrews:     6:1-5

# Chapter Eight
# LAWS OF SPIRITUAL HEALING

From my years of studying the Bible and the Edgar Cayce readings and applying them in my work with prayer, meditation, and healing, I have discovered some basic principles or spiritual laws of healing. Remember, we are defining healing as the process of becoming whole, becoming what we were created to be as children of God. It is interesting to note that the Greek verb that in most cases was the word translated in the New Testament as "being saved" could just as well be translated as "being healed."

The readings of Edgar Cayce are very Christocentric, i.e., they are Christ-oriented and Christ-centered. For some, this becomes a stumbling block. Yet if one can look beyond the words to the true meaning, it will be discovered that the emphasis is on the brotherhood of all men and the understanding that the Christ Consciousness is the awareness of the oneness of all and everything. Surely, Jesus perfectly demonstrated the love of God, the Christ, to all mankind; yet the Christ was and is present with all who teach and demonstrate the oneness of God throughout the world.

I. *Seek and Ye Shall Find:*

The first law is that we must seek in order to find ourselves in relation to God, beginning at some level to work with and claim Him, even as He has claimed us as His own. The best place to start is, of course, with one's own ideal:

> In the counsel at the present, then, keep ever before thee thy ideal in the Christ, for the healing, the counsel, the hope, the harmony, the peace that comes to all must come through that consciousness of the indwelling of that love in the experiences of all.                                           281-19

Each of us must be willing to look at his life and begin the cleansing process so that we can meet Him within the temple of our own being. We, too, must drink to the dregs the cup we have chosen, praying that we may measure up to the standard we have set for ourselves, and maintaining the attitude of "Not my will, but Thine, O Lord, be done in and through me."

*All* must pass under the rod as of that *cleansing* necessary for the inflowing of the Christ Consciousness, even as *He* passed under the rod, partook of the cup—and *gives* same to others.
281-5

Be not faint-hearted because failure seems to be in thy way, or that self falters—but "How many times shall I forgive, or ask forgiveness—seven times?" "Yea, seventy *times* seven!" or, "Not how I faltered, but did I seek His face again?" "Could ye not watch with me one hour?" The *man* crying out! "Sleep on, now, and take thy rest, for the hour cometh when I shall be even alone." So we find the changes, the weaknesses in the flesh—yet he that seeks shall find, and as oft as ye knock will the answer come. Seek to be one with Him, in body, in mind, in soul!
281-7

That which we seek in our growth is not self-development, but selfless development to the Christ Consciousness—selfless, because as this *awareness of the oneness* begins to dawn, selfishness is laid aside in the wisdom of knowing that only as there is unity, harmony, and peace for *all* does the individual soul find its fulfillment.

As given, each finds self most in the application of that it knows concerning the Father's and the Christ's ways in the hearts and lives of others. *Not so much self-development, but rather developing the Christ Consciousness in self, being selfless, that He may have HIS way with thee,* that He—the Christ—may direct thy ways, that He will guide thee in the things thou doest, thou sayest.
In this manner may one give of self to others most. Not as self-exaltation, but as glorifying the Christ that the Father may give those good gifts to those that love His ways. [author's italics]
281-20

The Christ Consciousness is a universal consciousness of the Spirit operative in the lives of all mankind. It is this awareness that brings healing.

II. *All Healing Comes from Within:*

Of all the laws relating to healing, this is the most inclusive and basic, yet perhaps the most difficult to understand and apply. It contains several sublaws, some of which are paradoxes. Specifically, within this great law are these components: 1) there must be the attunement that brings the healing; 2) faith is also needed to make healing possible; 3) no one heals anyone else; yet, in seeming contradiction to this, 4) by making the attunement within ourselves we can bring that attunement to others, and this will bring about healing; 5) we can't give what we don't have; but 6) we must be willing to give what we do have, for it is in helping others that we are healed; 7) we are or may become channels through whom the Spirit of God can flow; yet, 8) He doeth the work and giveth the increase.

## 1. Attunement is necessary.

We would almost go so far as to say that nothing and no one is healing in and of themselves, unless there is the response of the body consciousness to the outside influence. Whether the external impetus comes from drugs, surgery, osteopathy, massage, or chiropractic manipulation, unless there is the response of the life force within the body to that stimulus there can be no healing. In a reading specifically on laws of spiritual healing we find this statement:

For, as has been said oft, any manner in which healing comes—whether by the laying on of hands, prayer, by a look, by the application of any mechanical influence or any of those forces in *materia medica*—must be of such a nature as to produce that necessary within those forces about the atomic centers of a given body for it to bring resuscitating or healing.

The law, then, is compliance with the universal spiritual influence that awakens any atomic center to the necessity of its concurrent activity in relationships to other pathological forces or influences within a given body. Whether this is by spiritual forces, by any of the mechanical forces, it is of necessity one and the same.                                281-24

We find an elaboration of this in a reading for an epileptic child, indicating again the universal nature of the law.

You see, it is not that there are just so many treatments to be given and they can all be gotten through with and that's all there is to it! *NO application of ANY medicinal property or any mechanical adjustment, or any other influence, is healing of itself! These applications merely help to attune, adjust, correlate the activities of the bodily functions to nature and natural sources!*

*All healing, then, is from life! Life is God!* It is the adjusting of the forces that are manifested in the individual body . . .

The BODY is a pattern, it is an ensample of all the forces of the universe itself.

If all the rain that is helpful for the production of any element came at once, would it be better? . . .

It is the cooperation, the reaction, the response made BY the individual that is sought. Know that the soul-entity must find in the applications that response which attunes its abilities, its hopes, its desires, its purposes to that universal consciousness.

THAT is the healing—of any nature! . . .

. . . ATTUNE the body! [author's italics]           2153-6

2. Faith is essential.

Even Jesus, who was a manifestation of the very life of God, was not able to heal everyone. Remember, it was said of His work in Nazareth, "And He could do no mighty work there, except that He laid His hands upon a *few* sick people and healed them. And He marveled because of their unbelief." (Mark 6:5-6; author's italics) There is only one sin that is said to be unforgiveable: the sin against the Holy Spirit. My understanding of this is that as long as we deny the ability of the Spirit to be operative in our lives, it will not be, simply because God will not force us to become reconciled to Him. We are free to choose to remain alienated; and as long as we do, there can be no forgiveness, no allowing of the Spirit to flow. As soon as our hardness of heart is melted, we can be forgiven; i.e., His Spirit can then be operative within us to bring about healing or reconciliation. In Nazareth, as in all of the Holy Land, Jesus worked with and healed those who came seeking, who were open and receptive to what He had to give them.

During the Easter season of 1976, a holy man of India, Fakir Dayal, came to this country to teach and heal. Exorbitant claims about his healing ability were made by some of his followers, though not by the man himself. Many healings had been attributed to him in India, yet to my knowledge none were performed in the United States. I do not believe this says much about the attunement or lack of it within Fakir Dayal; I do think it says a great deal about the consciousness of those who gathered around him in this country. There was not the quickened response within the body-minds of those who needed healing, and thus they were unable to accept it within themselves.

Jesus said, "He who receives you receives me, and he who receives me receives Him who sent me. He who receives a prophet because he is a prophet shall receive a prophet's reward . . . " (Matt. 10:40-41) When we "receive a prophet in a prophet's name," it means that we have the consciousness needed to know within our heart of hearts that *he is a prophet;* we receive the reward of reaping a quickened Spirit. And if we then seek, we receive whatever it is we need. Another way of saying the same thing is, "According to your faith be it done to you." (Matt. 9:29)

We know that Jesus healed those who came to Him in faith, seeking His aid. Remember the interesting dialogue He had with the man who brought his son, who had a "dumb spirit," to Him for healing?

> "And Jesus asked his father, 'How long has he had this?' And he said, 'From childhood. And it has often cast him into the fire and into the water, to destroy him; but *if you can do anything,* have pity on us and help us.' And Jesus said to him, *'If you can! All things are possible to him who believes.'* Immediately the father of the child cried out and said, 'I believe; help my unbelief!'"
>
> (Mark 9:21-24; author's italics)

This man obviously wanted help for his son, but he had some doubts as to whether Jesus would be able to heal him. Jesus confronted him with this. We might interpret His reply as having a double meaning, each part of which is valid and in keeping with spiritual law. He seems to be saying, "You are questioning within yourself whether I am able to do this; yet I have perfect faith and am able. But *you* must have faith that it can be done. All things are possible for you, if you believe they are." The spirit was cast out, so there must have been a quickened response within both the son and the father.

This leads to another point, which we have not yet discussed: What about those who are mentally unable to seek help for themselves or too young to do so? They are in the keeping of relatives who are responsible for them, just as the afflicted person in the above passage was. Therefore the family is responsible for seeking help for them, and the faith of the family members may bring about a healing for the one who is troubled.

> ... "What ye ask in my name, believing, ye have already" if thou hast then prepared thy mind, *thy purpose and thy ideal being correct,* it is already thine. [author's italics]     2995-3

3. No one heals anyone else.

Each of us must come to the understanding that all the building and replenishing of the body proceeds from within and is the product of the life force within the individual responding to the external Universal forces.

*Q-7. Please give us a lesson on healing at this time.*
A-7. As has been outlined, well that each—in learning or experiencing that within self that would make for the abilities of healing—learn those things that acquaint self with the

divine forces that *are* Creative, and *those that are of HIS making, so that the healing is accredited to His force—even in self—wholly, even in that that is healed. These are the first principles, first causes—that all Life is in Him, and self only assists one seeking in becoming aware of that consciousness from within; for the kingdom (with all of its attributes) is from within.* As ye pray and meditate in Him, so does this arouse or awaken the consciousness in the experience of another that the healing may come; for there must flow out of self virtue (that is understanding), for HEALING to be accomplished in another. [author's italics]                                      281-10

There is such a temptation for the ego to become inflated when one is working with spiritual healing that it would be a good idea to make and hang on the wall a sign with this spiritual law printed boldly upon it: NO ONE HEALS ANYONE ELSE. This would stimulate us to respect the integrity of others, keeping us from being either busybodies or manipulators.

4. We must seek self-attunement in order to stimulate attunement within others.

Although no one heals anyone else, an individual or a group that has attuned itself sufficiently may quicken others so that the attunement will take place in them and stimulate the life force, producing healing. Our responsibility is to make and *keep* the attunement; the latter is the difficult part, because we so often just "pass through" a state of attunement. While we are "passing through" we may do some good, but the longer we are able to keep attuned, the more effective we will be in our service to others.

Here again, pride can enter, when we begin to think of ourselves as "holy people." We must remember that Jesus said of Himself, "Why callest thou me good? there is none good but...God." (Mark 10:18, KJV)

*Q-11....Please give us more information concerning the law of vibrations during meditation, and how we can understand and use that which we experience.*
A-11. As has been given, and as experienced by many, in opening self to the unseen forces about us, yet warred over by those influences save when in the presence of His influence, then as the forces are raised in self *know*—without doubt—there *are* His protecting influences, able, willing, capable, and *will* aid in that direction in which such vibrations, such influences, are raised to those individuals to whom they be directed, even by the spoken word; for, as is seen, as is understood by many, by most, that the *unseen* forces are the *active* forces, the *active* principles. That which *becomes* as a

99

manifestation is that which has been acted upon by those unseen forces and influences. What produces same? These are the vibrations to which a body has raised by its attunement of its whole being, its whole inner self, of a consciousness of that divine force that emanates in Life itself in this material plane. In sending such forces out, then, be mindful that there is no doubt that these will bring that as *He* sees fit, "Not my will, O Father, but Thine be done!" What did *this* bring to Him? The cross, the burdens, the crown of thorns—yet in its essence it brought those abilities to overcome death, hell and the grave. So, as in our raising ourselves to that understanding that His presence is guiding and directing those influences about those to whom we would direct His cause (for they have called on us), then *know* His will *is being* done in the manner as *thou* hast sent same to that individual!

Q-12. *Please give a definition of vibration in relation to healing.*

A-12. This would perhaps require several volumes to give a complete definition. Vibration is, in its simple essence or word, *raising* the Christ Consciousness in self to such an extent as it may flow *out* of self to him thou would direct it to. As, "Silver and gold I have none, but such as I have give I unto thee: In the *name* of Jesus Christ, stand up and walk!" *That* is an illustration of vibration that heals, manifested in a material world. What flowed out of Peter or John? That as received by knowing self in its entirety, body, mind, soul, is one *with* that Creative Energy that is LIFE itself! 281-7

In some sense the whole universe is energy vibrating at different rates, producing patterns of varying density. Man's body is surely an energy field, through which the Spirit-energy of another frequency—can move. The Edgar Cayce readings provide a great deal of information about vibration in relation to healing. The equation of vibration to the Christ Consciousness is completely understandable when we realize that the healing is brought about by the tuning in to the "awareness of the oneness" of our souls with God. The body is vibrating all the time; we become more and more aware of this when there is a stepping-up of the pattern as the attunement begins to take place.

To realize that the "*unseen* forces are the *active* forces, the *active* principles" and that that "which *becomes* as a manifestation is that which has been acted upon by those unseen forces and influences" takes a reorientation for most of us. But these are the principles of prayer and spiritual healing.

... the without and within are *one,* when the desires of the heart make each atom of the physical body vibrate with the consciousness of, the belief and the faith and the presence of, the Christ life, the Christ Consciousness. 5749-4

5. We cannot give what we do not have.

We understand this principle very well at the material level, but we are reluctant to apply it at the spiritual level. Perhaps our reluctance stems from an unwillingness to serve as instruments through whom the Spirit is operative. Surely God's bounty is endless and He can and at times does work regardless of our failure to fulfill our part in His plan; yet, if we want to be used by Him, we do have the responsibility of becoming more effective channels through which the Spirit can act.

**Would we heal others, we must first heal ourselves. 281-10**

*Q-12. What is the cause of the sensation I feel in my eyes at times during meditation?*
**A-12. As if manifest by the activities of those that would bring healing to others, the healing of every sort must come first in self that it may be raised in another. This is the healing in self, with that raising of the vision that may heal in others.**
**281-12**

We can raise the attunement in another only to the degree that we have been able to raise it within ourselves.

6. In helping others, we are healed.

At the same time that we reconize our own insufficiency, we need to raise our consciousness to the abundance that is God. So many people tell me, "Oh, I can't pray for anyone; it wouldn't do any good. God won't hear my prayers." Prayer is turning the conscious mind to the direction of the Spirit; it is the conscious tuning in to the spiritual forces of the universe. As we do this, we automatically put others in tune. The Bible tells us that the Spirit will pray for us, and it will; but we must be willing to be the channels through which the Spirit can flow.

In Jesus' teaching about the talents, the lesson is that when one uses what one has, more will be given. The conclusion of this parable is: "For to every one who has will more be given, and he will have abundance; but from him who has not, even what he has will be taken away." (Matt. 25:29) When we are willing to begin where we are with the little that we have and attempt to use it to God's glory, we will see an increase—in some cases tenfold, in some fiftyfold, in some one-hundred-fold. But when we do not use that which has been given, but bury it, even what we do have will be taken from us. Luke goes so far as to say: " . . . and from him who has not, *even what he thinks that he has* will be taken away." (Luke 8:18; author's italics)

It is only in giving that we set up the flow so that we may receive, but this must not be our motive for helping people. Any time something is done for self-glorification, we have already

101

received our reward in the praise we have sought from others. But when the action is motivated by love for God and fellow man, a flow is started that automatically comes back to us.

*Q-5. . . . Is it right to heal others when one has failed to accomplish healing in one's own life?*
A-5. Healing others is healing self. For, to give out that which aids others in reaching that which creates the perfect vibration of life in their physical selves, through the mental attitudes and aptitudes of the body, brings to self better understanding.
Yes, in healing others one heals self.
*Q-6. Should one meditate when not in a good physical condition?*
A-6. As we have given on prayer and meditation, when one can separate self sufficiently to be able to meditate *properly,* it is helpful. When one cannot, best not to attempt it.     281-18

There is a constant process in the flow of the Spirit. We work at making the attunement within ourselves that brings healing to us, and we send it out so that it may bring to others the attunement that will enable them to be healed. As their attunement is increased, it raises our attunement even higher, and so goes the flow.

Be thou mindful that thou may not know the love of thy God save as *thou* showest *His* love to thy brethren.     281-21

7. We are channels for the flow of the Spirit.

In the manners that have been outlined should there be the concerted effort of each to be a channel through which blessings may come to those who seek aid through them.
. . . Each, then, should strive the harder to be the channel, that those who seek in His name may not be disappointed in the manifestations of His love in their lives by the actions of those who have become negligent, or not in whole harmony with these efforts.
. . . All that strive gain in the manner as the effort is put forth. Remember that in His name *anything* may be accomplished that is in accord with His law.     281-8

We have the responsibility of doing all that we know to do that will enable us to be effective in our choice to be of service. We must cleanse the body, mind, and soul of all those things that would hinder, so that the attunement which we seek will manifest through us.
The word *channel* connotes something that is open at both ends. In applying this concept to spiritual healing, we indicate

that God is the supplier of the Spirit, which comes through our bodies and is directed by our minds to those we would aid. We begin the flow of the spiritual energy by our desire to be of help to those about us.

8. God does the work and gives the increase.

. . . though chosen as a channel, thou of thyself may do nothing. The Spirit of the Christ working in and through thee will bring the fruits of the Spirit in the experience of those that thou would lead to the light. In leading others thou gainest thyself.                                            281-19

Jesus emphasized this point again and again, even in relation to Himself, by saying that it was not He, but the Father in Him, that did the work. To keep a bridle on the ego and to meet the necessity of being anchored in God, it is imperative that we ever keep this law in the forefront of our consciousness.

It is possible to do a certain amount of healing by drawing upon the energies of the self. When this is done there will be depletion and illness, and if a person continues in this practice long enough, it may eventually kill him.

If the body in self is allowed to take on the condition and to be giving out those activities that are from other sources than the spiritual self, then it will become harmful for the body.
                                            3368-1

It is imperative to recognize that it is God who giveth the increase and that we do not have to "produce" anything. When we begin to feel that we must perform or bring about manifestations of healing in those we are concerned with aiding, we are completely off the track. When we are praying correctly there will be a release of all consequences, since we know that there will come to others that which they need.

III. *All Can Be Channels of Healing:*

*Q-2. . . . Should faith healing be included in the teachings of theology? If so, who is best qualified to teach it?*
A-2. There has been given by those in the orthodox manner those who SHOULD, THROUGH faith, laying on of hands, anointing with oil, praying over same. There is, in the broader sense, *that innate in each individual that may be awakened to those abilities in their activity,* are they willing to attune themselves to the laws as pertain to the active forces in self's OWN experience, keeping self unspotted and clean from the world, and KEEPING that that brings according in the body

that necessary for its awakening to its own spiritual activity.
Who shall do such? Such as are called in their own experience.
[author's italics]                                                    262-17

The motive, the desire, and the purpose are all equally
important in determining the direction of our service to others.
Since we are all children of God with the pattern of perfection
lying dormant within, when the awakening comes and we feel
the impetus to serve by healing, then the work must be begun·

IV. *God's Will Is Always for Our Good:*

. . . God hath not willed that any soul should perish but hath
with each temptation provided a way of approach.     281-25

Because of the mercy and grace of God, man finds himself in
the earth, free, or bound by his own past choices. He finds
himself subject to the laws of his heredity, his environment,
and his soul development (see 281-24). Regardless of the
condition in which we find ourselves physically, mentally, or
spiritually, we need always to realize that God's love for us is as
great as that He has for Jesus. And as any father realizes in
regard to his children, He knows that we are strengthened
when we endure with love that which we have to meet in the
earth.

" 'My son, do not regard lightly the discipline of the
Lord, nor lose courage when you are punished by
Him. For the Lord disciplines him whom He loves,
and chastises every son whom he Receives.'
"It is for discipline that you have to endure. God is
treating you as sons; for what son is there whom his
father does not discipline? If you are left without
discipline, in which all have participated, then you
are illegitimate children and not sons."
(Hebrews 12:5-8)

V. *Heal for the Purpose of Making the Body One with the
Whole:*

. . . the body spiritually must gain the proper relations as
must exist between the mental body, the physical body, and the
spiritual body. The application of the one without the other is
*not* the whole body. Hence in an entity there is the spiritual
body, there is the mental body, there is the physical body. To be
a physical healer, or a physician of the material body, without
a knowledge of the mental body, and without the *ability to
apply the spiritual force, there is expended just a part of*

104

After working with prayer and the laying on of hands for a number of years, the members of our Prayer Group became ever more convinced that the illnesses most of us want to heal are merely symptoms of greater dis-ease. And so it is that by and large we *do not* focus upon the manifested condition, but rather seek to bring the body-mind-soul into attunement. As this goal is worked toward, the symptoms will fall away and the soul itself will come into a better balance. Over a period of time, the real problem the soul is facing may come to consciousness so that it may be worked with at many levels of application.

VI. *All Illness Comes from Sin:*

... all illness comes from sin. This everyone must take whether they like it or not; it comes from sin—whether it be of body, of mind, or of soul ...                                     3174-1

Sin is a dirty word in our society, but basically it means a cutting off of ourselves from our real source of supply, God. Certainly all of us recognize that we live in a society where individuals are alienated one from another and most have no conception of a living relationship with the Father. When we begin to remedy that situation, our whole society will be on the road to greater health.

VII. *Group Action Is More Effective than Individual Action:*

God so loved the world that He did not send a committee; He sent the Christ—the Wayshower, the Life, and the Light of Men. However, because of Jesus' life and resurrection and the promised action of the Spirit in our lives, there is something very special about a group which gathers for the right purpose, seeking His presence and willing to do His work.

*Q-1. Is group action more effective than individual, and if so, why?*
*A-1.* "Where two or three are gathered in my name, I am in the midst of them." These words were spoken by Life, Light, Immortality, and are based on a law. For, in union is strength? Why?
Because as there is oneness of purpose, oneness of desire, it becomes motivative within the active forces or influences of a body. The multiplicity of ideas may make confusion, but added cords of strength in one become of the nature as to increase the *ability* and influence in every expression of such a law.
                                                                        281-24

There is a strengthening of mutual high purpose when a group of like-minded people come together with the same ideals and goals. There is the possibility of laying aside individual weaknesses and drawing on the strengths of one another. There is protection for each member, as well as a check on the egos of all. There is much greater power when a number of people work together in service to those who seek.

*Conclusion:*

. . . there is only *one* God, *one* Christ, one faith, one baptism; or as Christ hath given—this is the whole law; to love the Lord thy God with all thy mind, thy body, thy soul; thy neighbor as thyself. This is the whole law. This is wisdom. This is knowledge. Knowing that those things which have been put on through the activities of the elements within thine own forces of thy body and mind are but as the stepping-stones to the knowledge that no man, no number, no force, is above that knowledge that God is in and through *all*—and in Him ye live and move and have thy being. When this is fully comprehended, fully understood, ye have the working knowledge of God in the earth.                    281-34

## Bibliography

The five works listed below are relevant to material found throughout this book:

The Bible. The Revised Standard and King James versions have been used almost exclusively in this book.

*Meditation, Part I: Healing, Prayer and The Revelation* (The Prayer Group Readings). The Edgar Cayce Library Series, Vol. 2. Virginia Beach, Va.: Association for Research and Enlightenment, Inc., 1974.

*Meditation, Part II: Meditation, Endocrine Glands, Prayer, and Affirmations.* The Edgar Cayce Library Series, Vol. 3. Virginia Beach, Va.: Association for Research and Enlightenment, Inc., 1975.

*A Search for God,* Book I. Virginia Beach, Va.: Association for Research and Enlightenment, Inc., 1942, 1970.

*A Search for God,* Book II. Virginia Beach, Va.: Association for Research and Enlightenment, Inc., 1950.

The following books and articles relate to specific passages in the present work; they are listed according to the chapters to which they are most pertinent.

### Chapter I—"Meditation: A Way of Life"
Laubach, Frank C. *Prayer: The Mightiest Force in the World.* New York: Fleming H. Revell Company, 1946.

### Chapter II—"Affirmations"
Bro, Harmon Hartzell. *Edgar Cayce on Religion and Psychic Experience.* New York: Warner Books, Inc., Warner Paperback Library, 1970.

Puryear, Herbert B., and Thurston, Mark A. *Meditation and the Mind of Man.* Virginia Beach, Va.: A.R.E. Press, 1975.

Readings Research Department (A.R.E.), comp. *The Study Group Readings.* The Edgar Cayce Library Series, Vol. 7. Virginia Beach, Va.: Association for Research and Enlightenment, Inc., 1977. This series of readings was given for a small group of people who sought to become "a channel in presenting to the world the truth and light needed" (262-1); it answers their questions about prayer and meditation that arose over a thirteen-year period and is the best guide to prayer-group work that I know of.

### Chapter III—"Prayer Is Not a Technique"
Bro, Margueritte Harmon. *More Than We Are.* New rev. ed. New York: Harper & Row, Publishers, 1965.

Coburn, John B. *Prayer and Personal Religion.* Philadelphia: Westminster Press, Layman's Theological Library, 1957.

*A Commentary on the Book of the Revelation.* Virginia Beach, Va.: A.R.E. Press, 1969.

Elliott, Norman K. *How to Be the Lord's Prayer.* Westwood, N.J.: Fleming H. Revell Company, 1964.

Freer, Harold Wiley, and Hall, Francis B. *Two or Three Together: A Manual for Prayer Groups*. New York: Harper & Brothers, 1954. This book is excellent for groups who would not want to use the Cayce material. Its chapters are in the form of "meditations."

Heard, Gerald. *Ten Questions on Prayer*. Wallingford, Pa.: Pendle Hill, 1951.

Laubach. *Op. cit.*

Sanford, Agnes. *The Healing Light*. Saint Paul, Minn.: Macalester Park Publishing Company, 1947.

Verney, Stephen. *Fire in Coventry*. Westwood, N.J.: Fleming H. Revell Company, 1965. This is a good source for those just beginning prayer-group work, as it tells very explicitly how to start small groups within a Church.

Weatherhead, Leslie D. *Psychology, Religion and Healing*. New York: Abingdon-Cokesbury Press, 1951.

**Chapter V—"Why Work in a Prayer Group?"**

Cayce, Hugh Lynn. *Gifts of Healing*. Virginia Beach, Va.: A.R.E. Press, 1973.

*Meditation*. Circulating File. Virginia Beach, Va.: Association for Research and Enlightenment, Inc., 1977.

Puryear and Thurston. *Op. cit.*

Puryear, Meredith Ann. "A Philosophy of Healing." *The A.R.E. Journal*, Vol. VI, No. 5 (September, 1971), pp. 173-182.

*The Study Group Readings. Op. cit.*

Woodward, Mary Ann. *That Ye May Heal*. Rev. ed. Virginia Beach, Va.: A.R.E. Press, 1974.

**Chapter VII—"Healing Through the Laying On of Hands"**

Moss, Thelma, and Johnson, Kendall. "Your Color Aura." *House and Garden*, September, 1975, p. 102.